MW01618580

How to Read Hieroglyphics & Ancient Egyptian Art

Authored By

Bernard Paul Badham

Student Edition

kemetscribe.com

ARK PUBLISHING

Ameni-amenna

First published in Great Britain in 2019 by Ark Publishing
www.arkpublishing.co.uk

Series title list: www.kemetscribe.com
Series title code: KS No.001.

Student Edition

ISBN-13: 978-1912418008

Author

Bernard Paul Badham

Egyptologist, Author and Physicist. Born in Wales in 1950 Bernard has worked as a school and college lecturer and as the Head of Science at the British International School in Cairo from where he explored the ancient sites of Egypt for over a decade. Bernard is the author of many Egyptology publications and has created a series for students to learn how to read Ancient Egyptian Hieroglyphics from foundation course to more advanced studies and exercises.

Hieroglyphic Sign List & Vocabulary

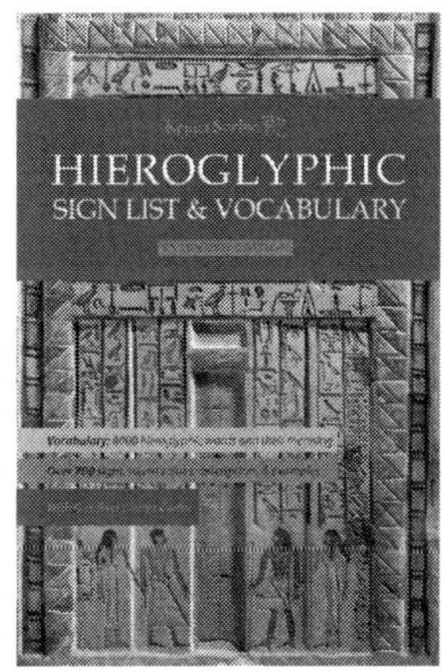

Translate hieroglyphic signs and words using an efficient page index for a two-part sign list with over 700 signs, sound values, descriptions and examples and an extended vocabulary of 4000 hieroglyphic words and thier meaning. An essential study tool for the student of Egyptian hieroglyphics allowing quick sign list and vocabulary reference for transliteration and translation.

ISBN: 9781912418060

A Concise Chronicle of the Kings and Queens of Ancient Egypt

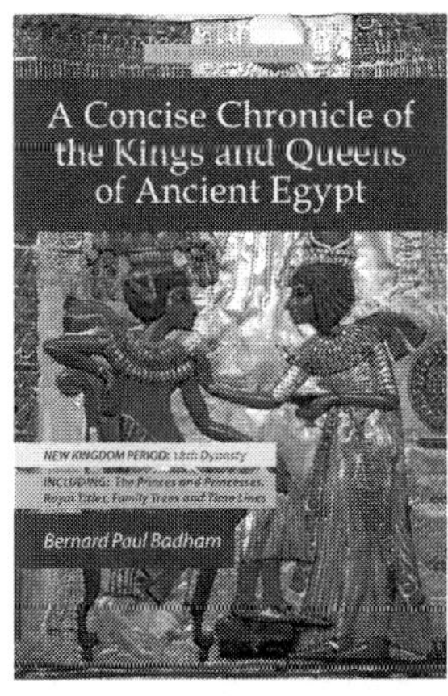

A Concise Chronicle of the Kings and Queens of Ancient Egypt including the Princes and Princesses, Royal Titles, Family Trees and Time Lines. Students of Egyptology and Hieroglyphics will find the book valuable as a quick reference guide to one of the most interesting dynasties of Ancient Egypt.

ISBN: 9781912418107

Important Note

The method of this book is that the student should learn the main principles of writing by simple mechanical learning. Grammar, sentence structure and word order should be learned through use and examples, much in the same way a child learns his own native language. Learning at an early age comes by listening, mimicking and by repetition, a child does not need to learn that in English the adjective (red) precedes the noun (book) as in: 'the red book,' the child hears the word order and simply repeats what he has heard. The student should do likewise and learn by repetition of use.

The main exercises in this book concentrate on phonetic spelling, vocabulary and translation from the hieroglyphic to English. The student will not be required to translate from English to Egyptian as this involves much learning of grammatical rules. Some grammar *is* used in this book, but it is kept to a minimum. In the examples and exercises (and in real inscriptions) the scribe has already written the signs in the correct word order and used the correct grammar, it is only necessary therefore that the student learns how to translate into English.

The key to learning any language is vocabulary, and therefore the student should commit to memory new words and sound and idea signs as one makes progress through the lessons. For reference during the process of translation, where memory fails, the student should refer to the Kemet Scribe Sign List & Vocabulary Extended Edition (hieroglyphic dictionary) and for further study, Sir Alan Gardiner's *Egyptian Grammar*. In Gardiner's book the student will find an in-depth study into Egyptian grammar and a list of signs with their phonetic values and meanings and an Egyptian to English Dictionary.

To aid memory the student should write their own notes as the lessons progress and learn to draw the signs in a stylised short-hand form, carefully replicating the identifying shapes of the signs.

Bernard Paul Badham

Contents

Section II
Reading Ancient Egyptian Art

Appendix

Answers to Exercises

KEY DEFINITIONS

Student Scribe:

Transliterate: Not to be confused with Translation. Transliteration is a type of conversion of a text from one script to another that involves swapping letters; to transcribe a word from one type of alphabet into corresponding letters of another alphabet. Transliteration is not primarily concerned with representing the sounds of the original but rather with representing the characters.

Transposition: Removal from one place to another, to change the relative position, order, or sequence of; cause to change place.

Phonetic: Phonetic means relating to the sound of a word. Concerning speech sounds, their production and combination, and their representation by written symbols.

Phonogram: The word phonogram is translated as the "written symbol for a sound". Phono meaning sound and gram meaning symbol. Any written symbol standing for a sound, syllable, morpheme, or word or a sequence of written symbols having the same sound in a variety of different words.

Monogram: A design consisting of two or more symbols (hieroglyphs) combined or interlaced to make one design.

Ideogram: An ideogram is a sign or a graphic symbol representing an object, concept or idea without expressing, as in a phonetic system, the sounds that form its name. (E.g. %, @, &, etc). Some ideograms are comprehensible only by familiarity with prior convention; others convey their meaning through pictorial resemblance to a physical object, and thus may also be referred to as pictograms.

Particles: Particles are words which do not fit into the usual grammatical definitions, they add meaning or emphasis, such as 'behold', 'lo', 'when', 'now' etc. In the sentence "I tidied up the room", the adverb "up" is a particle.

Determinatives: When an ideogram ends the word it is classed as a determinative: it determines the meaning of the word.

Biliteral: Biliteral Signs are duel sound symbols which represent a specific sequence of two consonants, also two vowels, or combinational of both.

Triliteral: Triliteral Signs are triple sound symbols which represent a specific sequence of three consonants, also three vowels, or combinational of both.

Juxtaposition: An act or instance of placing close together or side by side, especially for comparison or contrast.

Demonstratives: Demonstratives are words that show which person or thing is being referred to. In the sentence: 'This is my house', 'this' is a demonstrative. The demonstratives in English are this, that, these, and those.

Preposition: A preposition is a word such as after, in, to, on, and with. Prepositions are usually used in front of nouns or pronouns and they show the relationship between the noun or pronoun and other words in a sentence.

Vocative: A word or phrase used to address a reader or listener directly, usually in the form of a personal name, title, or term of endearment. In speech, the vocative is indicated by intonation.

Negation: The action or logical operation of negating or making negative. Such as a refusal or denial of something. If your friend thinks you owe him a pint of beer and you say that you don't, your statement is a negation.

Cardinal and Ordinal: A Cardinal Number is a number that says how many of something there are, such as one, two, three, four, five. An Ordinal Number is a number that tells the position of something in a list, such as 1st, 2nd, 3rd, 4th, 5th etc.

Syntax: Syntax is the set of rules, principles, and processes that govern the structure of sentences in a language. Such as the way in which words and punctuation are used and arranged to form phrases, clauses and sentences.

Noun: A noun is a part of speech that names a person, place, thing, idea, action or quality. All nouns can be classified into two groups of nouns, either common or proper. Proper nouns refer to the individual name of a person, place or thing.

Pronoun: A pronoun is a word that takes the place of a noun. In the sentence Jim saw Jenny, and he waved at her, the pronouns he and her take the place of Jim and Jenny, respectively. (I, me, he, she, herself, you, it, that, they, each, few, many, who, whoever, whose, someone, everybody, etc.) The replacement noun is called the antecedent.

Dependent Pronouns: Dependent Pronouns are separate but never stand alone at the beginning of a sentence.

Independent Pronouns: Independent Pronouns almost always stand at the beginning of a sentence.

Suffix-Pronouns: They are suffix pronouns because (in hieroglyphs) they follow, and are affixed to preceding words. Suffix pronouns are attached to nouns, verbs, prepositions. These signs are mostly used to represent personal possession (possessives) in phrases such as: my book, your book, his/her book, our book, their book.

Plural: A word or form consisting, containing, or pertaining to more than one. Nouns can be either singular or plural. Singular means just one of the person, animal or thing which the noun refers to. Plural means more than one.

Adjectives: An adjective is a word that describes, identifies or further defines a noun or a pronoun.

Possessive Adjective: A possessive adjective is an adjective that is used to show ownership. It comes before a noun in the sentence and lets us know to whom the noun belongs.

Superlative: An adjective that expresses that the thing or person being described has more of the certain quality than anything or anyone else of the same type: "Wisest" is the superlative of "wise".

Roman Numerals

The modern student of hieroglyphs should know how to read Roman numerals as they are universally used to chronologically categorize the Royal Dynasties of Ancient Egypt. It is not required for the lessons in this book but you can easily learn how to read them using the rules below:

I = 1 **V** = 5 **X** = 10 **L** = 50 **C** = 100 **D** = 500 **M** = 1000

Roman numerals consist of a combination of the **I, V, X, L, C, D** and **M** letters. The position of the letters in relationship to each other (before or after) is what determines the total numerical value of the Roman numeral (letter combination).

For example:

If a smaller number (**I**) follows a larger number (**X**), the numbers are added.

For example, the Roman numeral **XII** is the addition of ten (**X**) and two (**II**), resulting in the value of twelve. **XII** = 10 + 2 = 12

If a smaller number is before a larger number, the smaller number is subtracted from the larger.

For example, the Roman numeral **IIX** calls for the subtraction of two (**II**) from ten (**X**), resulting in the value of eight. **IIX** = 10 - 2 = 8

More examples:

VIII = 5 + 3 = 8
IX = 10 - 1 = 9
XXIV = 10 + 10 + (5 - 1) = 24
XL = 50 - 10 = 40
XC = 100 - 10 = 90
MCMLXXX = 1000 + (1000 - 100) + 50 + 30 = 1980

Hieroglyphic Note Book

Use A5 and pocket size notebooks for frequent practice to train your memory. Use a black liquid ink pen or a technical drawing pen and develop your technique to replicate and draw each hieroglyph with as few strokes as possible.

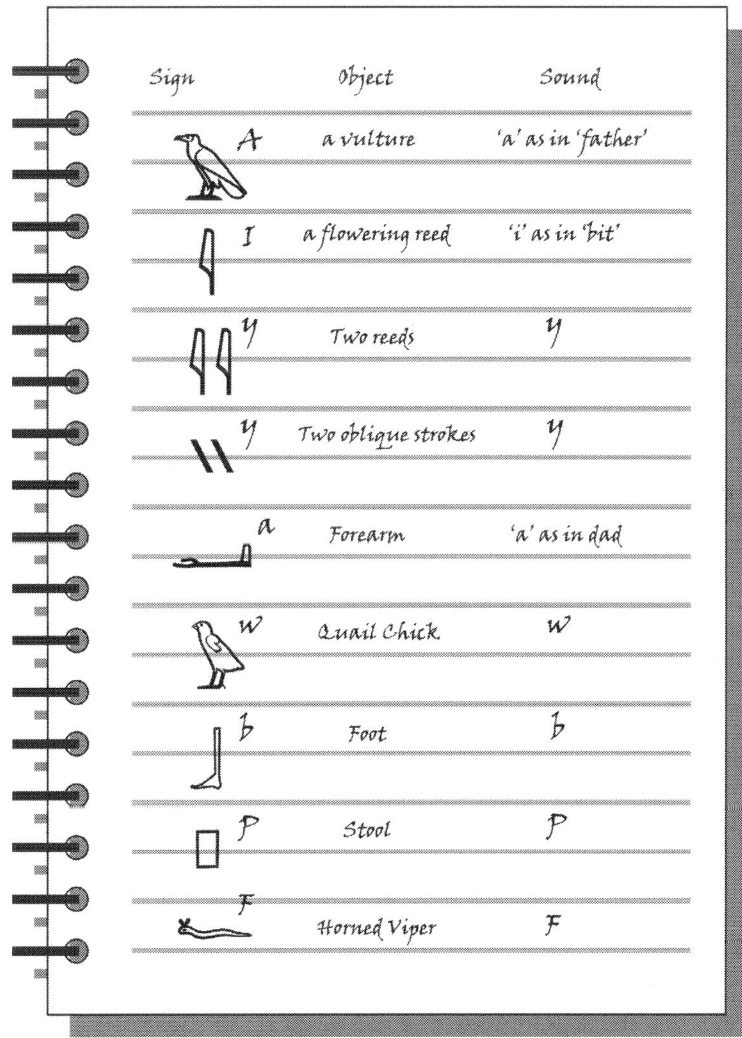

Introduction

The Language of Ancient Egypt

mdw-nTr

Pronounced 'Medew-Netjer'

'God's Words'

The Egyptian hieroglyphs, the **mdw-nTr**, 'Gods Words', was the writing system used by the ancient Egyptians that combined ideograms (idea signs) and phonetic (sound) signs including an alphabetic list of signs. Egyptians used simpler cursive hieroglyphs for religious literature on papyrus and wood. Hieroglyphs are related to two other Egyptian scripts, hieratic and demotic. Early hieroglyphs date back as far as 3,300 BCE, and continued to be used up until about 400 CE, when non-Christian temples were closed and their monumental use was no longer necessary. After the loss of the knowledge of hieroglyphic writing, the decipherment of hieroglyphs remained an enduring puzzle which would only be solved in the 1820s by Jean-Francois Champollion, with the help of the Rosetta Stone.

The term 'God's Words' refers to the divine nature of their origin, the god Thoth (Djhwty) is ascribed with giving the early ancient Egyptians, during the primordial formation times, the gift of writing: the hieroglyphic writing system.

Thoth the God of Writing

Thoth was the patron saint of the scribe. In the following scene we see Nefertari coming before the god Thoth requesting the ability to read and write in the afterlife. In between them stands his scribe's palette.

Her titles read:

How it sounds: **nsw Hmt wrt, nbt tAwy (nfr-itry, mrt n mwt) mAa-xrw xr nTr aA**

Literal translation: king's wife great, lady two-lands (beautiful-lady, beloved of Mut-Goddess), true-voice, under god great

FULL TRANSLATION: 'King's Great Wife, Lady of the Two Lands (Egypt), Nefer-itry, beloved of the goddess Mut, True of Voice, under the great god'

The use of the hieroglyphic sacred texts of ancient Egypt originated around 3150 BC in its simplest form from evidence found in mudbrick tombs to its final recorded use by the priests at the temple of Philae in around 430AD.

The development of the language during this time depends on whether one is considering the spoken, daily secular written texts or the sacred hieroglyphic texts inscribed in stone and written on papyrus, the latter changed little during the whole period of Egyptian pharaonic history and much of the changes which did occur happened during the late Ptolemaic period.

The different development stages of the language:

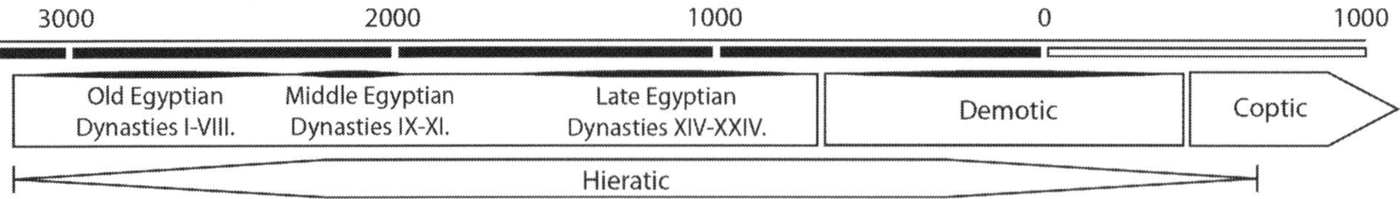

Old Egyptian: Dynasties I-VIII. 3180-2240 BC. Mainly the inscribed Pyramid Texts.

Middle Egyptian: Dynasties IX-XI. 2240-1990 BC. Monumental texts.

Late Egyptian: Dynasties XIV-XXIV. 1573-715 BC. Business documents and letters.

Demotic: 715 BC – 470 AD. Books and documents.

Coptic Script: Third century AD onwards. Language spoken and written by the Christian Copts, the Christian descendants of the ancient Egyptians, in whose churches it is read, though not understood, even to the present day.

Hieratic Script: The **Hieroglyphic** script remained throughout the history of Pharaonic Egypt when pertaining to sacred priestly texts inscribed on monuments, the hieratic script used for sacred texts written on papyri became more and more cursive; an early version of short hand.

For daily secular use the **Hieratic** gave way to an even more short hand version of the hieratic, the **Demotic**, where the original forms of the hieroglyphic were almost completely lost. The three following examples of texts show the cursive development of the written texts:

1. 12th Dynasty: **Literary Hieratic** with **hieroglyphic** transcription:

2. 12th Dynasty: **Official Hieratic** with **hieroglyphic** transcription:

3. **Literary Demotic** of the third century BC with **hieroglyphic** transcription.

SECTION I

READING HIEROGLYPHICS

LESSON 1

1.1 Direction of Writing

Hieroglyphic inscriptions occur in columns and horizontal rows. With horizontal rows they are read from the left or the right depending on the direction the hieroglyphs face.

The row below must be read from left to right since the persons, birds, animals and objects are facing the left.

Within groups of hieroglyphs upper has presidence over lower. Thus, in the following line:

The order of the above signs, left to right, is:

Hieroglyphs in columns are read from top to bottom. Here is an inscription written in four possible ways. The numbers give the reading order of individual hieroglyphs:

For maximum use of space and artistic symmetry the artist arranges groups of hieroglyphs in squares:

1.2 Sound Signs/Phonograms

Sound signs are called phonograms and there are three types, those which carry a single consonant sound as in the alphabetic signs, and those which carry two or three consonant sounds.

Single Sound Signs: f r b

Dual Sound Signs: mn pr aA

Triple Sound Signs: nfr Htp xpr

1.3 Alphabetic Sound Signs

The following list of alphabetic signs should be learned as soon as possible as they form the basis of hieroglyphic transliteration into English sound letters and the alphabetic order in which they are portrayed follows the order of ancient Egyptian hieroglyphic dictionaries.

Sign	Translit.	Object	Sound
𓄿	**A**	vulture	a as in father
𓇋	**i**	flowering reed	i or y as in yid
𓇌	**y**	two reeds	y
𓏭	**y**	two oblique strokes	y
𓂝	a	forearm	a as in dad
𓅱	**w**	quail chick	w
𓃀	**b**	foot	b
𓊪	**p**	stool	p
𓆑	**f**	horned viper	f
𓅓	**m**	owl	m
𓈖	**n**	water	n
𓂋	**r**	mouth	r
𓉔	**h**	reed shelter	h

Sign	Translit.	Object	Sound
	H	twisted flax	emphatic, aspirated h
	x	sieve	kh, like ch in Scottish 'loch'
	X	animal's belly with teats	kh, like ch in German 'ich'
	s (z)	door bolt	hard s
	s	fold of cloth	s
	S	pool	sh
	q	hill slope	q
	k	basket with handel	k
	g	jar stand	g
	t	loaf of bread	t
	T	tethering rope	tj, tsh
	d	hand	d
	D	snake	dj

Later alternative forms for alphabetic sounds

w **n** **m** t, **ti**

Practical Exercise Guide

Use an A4 lined and margined exercise book and a black pen to complete the exercises at the end of each lesson. Use a red pen for corrections and to self-mark your exercises in the margin area.

The <u>answers</u> to all of the exercises are in the appendix.

A4 Practical Exercise Example

< Self-mark your exercises here >

Kemet Scribe

Lesson 1

Exercise 1 Vocabulary 1

a)

m in, by means of, with, from, out of

n to, for

r to, into, towards, in respect of

pn this (masculine and follows its noun)

tn this (feminine and follows its noun)

ky other, another (masc. precedes its noun)

kt other, another (fem. precedes its noun)

im there, therein, therefrom, therewith

bw place

EXERCISE 1

Vocabulary (Part 1)

a) Learn and write out from memory the following words in hieroglyphs, with transliteration and meaning:

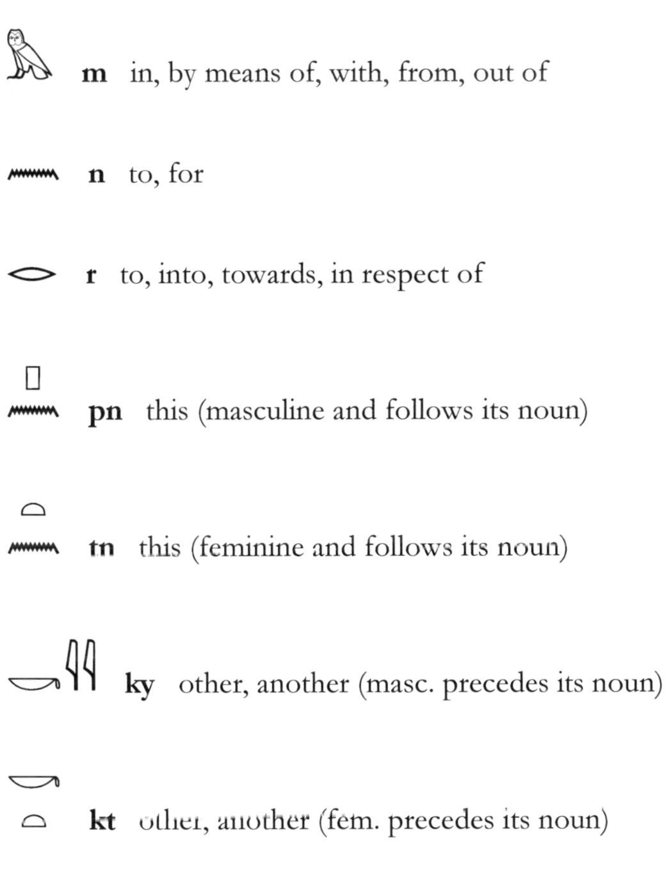

m in, by means of, with, from, out of

n to, for

r to, into, towards, in respect of

pn this (masculine and follows its noun)

tn this (feminine and follows its noun)

ky other, another (masc. precedes its noun)

kt other, another (fem. precedes its noun)

im there, therein, therefrom, therewith

bw place

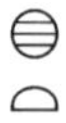

xt thing

ptH the name of the god Ptah

iw is, are, behold

rn name

Dd say, speak

Hna together with

b) Write in hieroglyphs the following combination of letters:

hn arq grH sfT ptr my Xrd iAx wiA Dsf qnd ptpt wSb Tsm

Study Note

Before proceeding remember to use your notebook to practice the **alphabetic sound signs** in lesson one. Repetition is key: by repeatedly hand drawing the signs in a stylised short-hand form with their transliteration and sound you will gradually embed them in to your memory. Use up as many notebooks as you can when studying as repetition will also help you to develop your own hieroglyphic drawing technique.

LESSON 2

2.1 Ideograms

Ideograms are signs which carry a meaning pictorially:

1. **The Sun:** ☉ ideas: sun, light, time, day

Example examples of use:

ra light, time, day, **hrw** day, **rk** time,

wbn rise, shine

2. **A Boat:** ideas: boat, ship, sacred bark, sail

Examples of use:

dpt boat, **wiA** solar/sacred bark,

xd fare downstream

3. **Scribe's Apparatus**: ideas: scribe's apparatus of water pot, pen holder and pallete: scribe, write, smooth

Examples of use:

sS write, **sS** scribe, **naa** smooth, finely ground

4. **Animal's Ear**: ideas: animal's ear: death, listen

Examples of use:

sDm hear, listen, **sDm** be death

2.2 Determinatives

When an ideogram ends the word it is classed as a **determinative**: it determines the meaning of the word. Determinatives are useful for knowing where a word ends. The seated man in the word for 'scribe' acts as a determinative. The following list of generic determinatives should be learned over time:

man,

people,

or god, king,

or goddess, queen

praise, adoration

eat, drink, think, speak, feel

weary, tired, weak

enemy, death

mummy, likeness, shape

hair, mourn, forlorn

woman,

child

god, king

high, rejoice, support

force, effort

lift, carry,

enemy, foreigner

or lie down, death, bury

head, nod, throttle

eye, see, actions of the eye

actions, conditions of the eye

ear, states of activities of the ear

or force, effort, strike

arm, bend, arm, cease

phallus, beget, urinate

walk, run, go, come-forth

limb, flesh

bodily discharges

savage

bird, insect

fish

tree

marshland

vine, fruit, garden

corn

sky, above

nose, smell, joy, contempt

tooth, actions of teeth

offer, present

embrace, envelop

leg, foot, actions of feet

walk backwards, return

tumours, odours, disease

or cattle

skin, mammal

small, bad, weak

serpent, snake, worm

lotus pool, meadow

plant, flower

wood, tree

grain

sun, light, time

night, darkness

fire, heat, cook

copper, bronze

water, liquid, actions of water

irrigated land

road, travel, position

foreign

house, building

box, coffin

boat, ship, navigation

clothe, linen

rope, actions with rope

hoe, cultivate, hack up

cup

beer, vessel, measure

loaf, cake, offering

star

stone

sand, minerals, pellets

or body of water

land

desert, foreign country

town, village, Egypt

door, open

shrine, palanquin, mat

sacred bark

bind, document

knife, cut

break, divide, cross

vessel, anoint

bread, cake

festival

book, writing, abstract words

royal name, king

I one, the object depicted

I I I several, plural

several, plural

o o o several, plural

substitute for difficult signs

When ideograms stand for the actual objects they depict usually the phonetic signs are not shown and the object is followed by a single stroke. If the noun object is feminine the letter t precedes the stroke:

ra 'sun' **niwt** 'town, city' **Axt** 'horizon' **Hr** 'face'

The use of the stroke was extended to phonetic ideograms:

sA 'son' **s** 'man'

In Egyptian there are two genders, masculine as in **ra** 'sun' and feminine as in **niwt** 'town, city,' the feminine ends with the letter **t**.

The feminine for **s** 'man' being **st** 'woman':

st 'woman'

Note: most masculine words probably ended with a **w** which were omitted for simplicity of writing, thus the feminine ended was **wt**. It is quite likeky therefore that the original sound of the words for man and woman were:

sw 'man' **swt** 'woman'

2.3 Sentences

Sentence structure in ancient Egyptian hieroglyphic writing is best learned by syntax, where the word order is learned by use, much like a child learns the word order in language by mimicry. In English we place the describing word (adjective) before the naming word (noun), as in the 'red book'; in ancient Egyptian the reverse is true: 'book red.'

The following examples of hieroglyphic sentences are given where the word order of **literal translation** should be written followed by the natural English word order in **full translation**:

Transliteration (sounds): **wbn ra m pt**

Literal Translation (word order preserved): rises sun in sky

Full Translation (English): 'The sun rises in the sky'

rx sS sxr m hrw pn know scribe counsel in day this 'The scribe knows a counsel on this day'

ra im Ra therein 'Ra is there'

To introduce sentences the word (enclitic particle) **iw** is often used: **iw** 'behold, is, are'

iw ra m pt behold/is ra in sky 'The sun *is* in the sky' or '*Behold* is the Ra in Sky'

wbn ra iw tA m rSwt rises sun is earth in joy 'When the sun rises, the earth is in joy (rejoices)'

VOCABULARY 2

Learn and write out from memory the following words in hieroglyphs, with transliteration and meaning:

rx 'become acquainted with, know'

xm 'not know, be ignorant of'

gr 'be silent, cease'

xd 'fare downstream'

gr 'go down, descend'

sDm 'to hear'

wbn 'rise, shine'

ra 'sun, day'

ra 'sun, day'

ra 'Ra, the sun god'

iaH 'moon'

tA 'land, earth'

pt 'heaven, sky'

sxr 'plan, counsel'

hrw 'day, day-time'

grH 'night'

rSwt 'joy, gladness'

dpt 'boat, ship'

wiA 'ship, sacred bark'

nDs poor man, commoner'

s 'man'

st 'woman'

sS 'scribe'

Axt 'horizon'

pr **'**house'

niwt 'town, city'

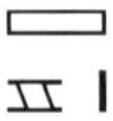

S 'lake, pool'

Study Note

Before proceeding use your notebook to practice the **determinative signs** in lesson 2.2. Repetition is key: by repeatedly hand drawing the signs in a stylised short-hand form with thier meaning you will gradually embed them in to your memory. Use up as many notebooks as you can when studying as repetition will also help you to develop your own hieroglyphic drawing technique.

EXERCISE 2

Transliterate and translate:

1.

2.

3.

4.

5.

6.

7.

8. 

9. 

■ An Important Note ■

Whether translating from hieroglyphs to English, translate no more than three signs/literal words at a time, this approach will break down the sentence into easily manageable groups of words (phrases) where the word order and meaning can be established before composing the whole sentence. You will notice in the answers section I have separated these phrases during translation with commas.

LESSON 3

3.1 Biliteral (Dual Sound) Signs

Learning the Egyptian alphabet is essential for translating hieroglyphs, as is learning the dual sound signs called biliterals. Below is a list of biliteral signs ending with the sound **A**:

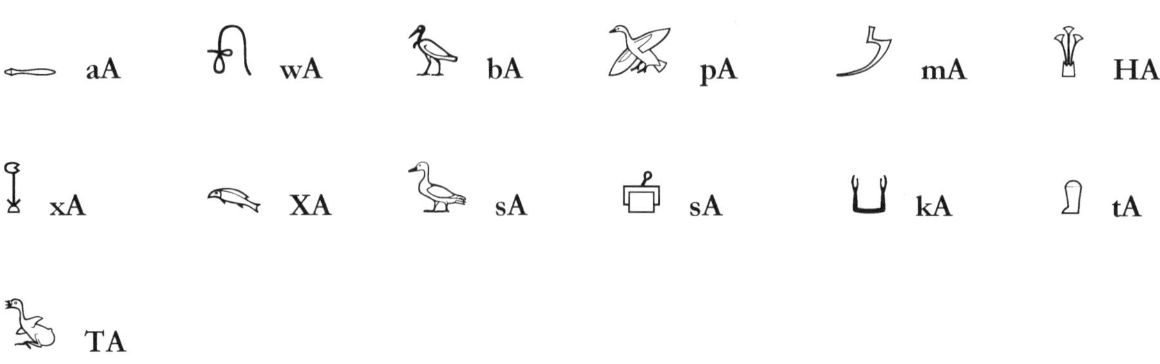

3.2 Phonetic Complements

The biliteral and triliteral signs are almost always accompanied by expressing part or all of their sound value using phonetic complements. These phonetic complements are not written down in transliteration, they are present only for clarity of the sound to be expressed as some biliterals and triliterals have two sound values:

sound values: **mr, Ab**

Phonetic complements are used with the above biliteral to determine the sound value of the word: **mr** or **Ab**:

mr 'be ill' **Ab** 'desire'

Further examples of the use of phonetic complements:

SA **bA**

3.3 Personal Pronouns

Suffix-Pronouns

The first group of signs in this class are called **suffix-pronouns**; these signs are used to represent personal **possession** in phrases such as: my book, your book, his/her book, our book, their book. In transliteration these sounds are preceded by a full stop:

masculine			feminine		
	.i	I, me, my		.i	I, me, my
	.k	you, yours		.T	you, yours
	.f	he, him, his, it, its		.s	she, her, hers, it, its

Neutral Plural

	.n(w)	we, us, our
	.Tn(w)	you, your
	.sn(w)	they, them, their
	.w	they, them, their

Dual

	.ny	we two, us two, our
	.Tny	you two, your
	.sny	they two, them two, their

Examples of use of suffix-pronouns:

pr.f town.his 'his town'

niwt.sn(w) town.their 'their town'

n.i to.me 'to me'

Hna.s together-with.her 'together with her'

Dd.k speak.you 'you speak'

sDm.T hear.you 'you hear'

Note: the above examples take on the form **sDm.f** 'he listens' and are translated in the present tense.

The **sDm.n.f** form is translated as past tense, 'he heard':

sDm.n.f heard.of.he 'he heard' (masculine)

sDm.n.T heard.of.you 'you heard' (feminine)

Changing the suffix-pronouns to include the reflective 'myself', 'yourself' etc. is achieved by adding the sign: **Ds**:

ra.Ds.f ra.self.him 'Ra himself'

Use of the enclitic particle **iw** 'behold, is, are' with suffix-pronouns:

iw.n(w), m pr.f is/are.we, in house.his 'we are in his house' or 'behold, we are in his house'

3.4 The 'm' of Predication

Use of the preposition **m** to indicate the meaning 'in the postion of, as':

iw.k, m sS behold/is/are.you, as scribe 'you are a scribe' or 'you are in the position of scribe' or you are as a scribe'

iw, nDs, pn m sS is/are, poor man, this as scribe 'this poor man is (as/in the position of) a scribe'
Use of the word **tw** meaning 'one, you':

sDm.tw, r pn hear.one,/you, utterance this 'one hears this utterance'

sDm.tw.f hear.one.him/it 'One hears it or it is heard'

rx.tw.f know.one.he 'he is known'

Note: in the use of **.tw**, often it is abbreviated by dropping the **w** to give **.t**

Further examples of the use **.tw** with suffix-pronouns:

sDm.i hear.I 'I hear'

sDm.tw.i hear.one.I 'I am heard'

sDm.k hear.you 'you hear' (masc.)

sDm.tw.k hear.one.you 'you are heard' (masc.)

sDm.T hear.you 'you hear' (fem.)

sDm.tw.T hear.one.you 'you are heard' (fem.)

sDm.f hear.he/it 'he/it hears'

sDm.tw.f hear.one.he/it 'he/it is heard'

sDm.s hear.she/it 'she/it hears'

sDm.tw.s hear.one.she/it 'she/it is heard'

sDm.n(w) hear.we 'we hear'

sDm.tw.n(w) hear.one.we 'we are heard'

sDm.Tn(w) hear.you 'you hear' (plur.)

sDm.tw.Tn(w) hear.one.you 'you are heard' (plur.)

sDm.sn hear.they 'they hear'

sDm.tw.sn hear.one.they 'they are heard'

sDm.tw hear.one 'one hears'

Examples of the use of suffix pronouns using the verb 'to say':

Dd.s, n.f say.she, to.him 'she says to him'

Dd n.f, sS say to.him scribe 'the sribe says to him'

Dd.tw, n.f, r pn say.one, to.him, utterance this 'This utterance is said to him'

Use of the enclitic particle **grt** meaning 'now, moreover':

iw, grt, ra m pt is/are, now/moreover, sun in sky 'now the sun was in the sky'

Use of the word **in** meaning 'by':

Dd.tw, r pn, in s say.one, utterance this, by man 'This utterance is said by a man'

hAb.k, sS, Dd.f, sxr.k send.you, scribe, says.he, plan.your 'You send the scribe, he says your plan'

Use of the word **ix** meaning 'now, then, therefore':

ix, Dd sr then/now, say official 'Then the official will say'

ix, Dd.k, n sA.k then, say.you, son.your 'Then you will say to your son'

VOCABULARY 3

Learn and write out from memory the following words in hieroglyphs, with transliteration and meaning:

mAA 'see'

DA 'cross, ferry across'

rS 'be glad, rejoice'

hAb 'send'

sA 'son'

sAt 'daughter'

it 'father' **Note**: the viper glyph is used here as an ideogram

bAk 'male servant'

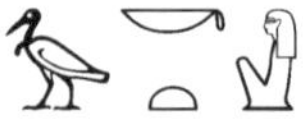

bAkt 'female servant'

wAt 'road, way, side'

xA 'office, hall, diwan'

kAt 'construction, work, device'

TAt 'vizier'

aA 'donkey, ass'

StA 'secret'

itrw 'river'

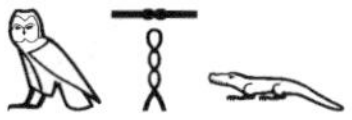

msH 'crocodile'

r(A) 'mouth, utterance'

Hr 'face, sight'

Hr 'upon, in, at from, on account of, through, and, do, from, after, concerning, because of'

m 'in, with, from, as, in the position of'

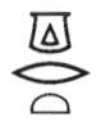

grt 'now, moreover'

in 'by, so says'

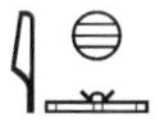

ix 'now, then, therefore'

tw 'one, you, this, that'

iw 'behold, is, are

im 'in, with, from, as, therein'

Study Note

Before proceeding use your notebook to practice the **vocabulary signs** in lessons 1 and 2. Repetition is key: by repeatedly hand drawing the signs in a stylised short-hand form with thier transliteration and meaning you will gradually embed them in to your memory. Use up as many notebooks as you can when studying as repetition will also help you to develop your own hieroglyphic drawing technique.

EXERCISE 3

Transliterate and translate:

1.

2.

3.

4.

5.

6.

7.

8.

9.

LESSON 4

Dependent Pronouns

4.1 Biliteral Signs

We start this lesson by learning more biliteral (dual sounding) signs:

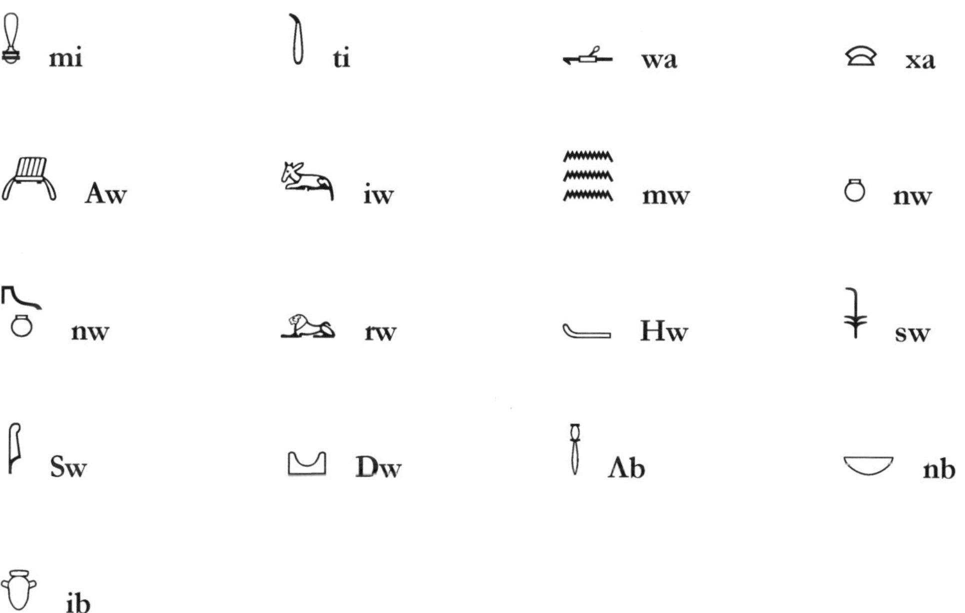

4.2 Triliteral (Triple Sound) Signs

Some signs act as phonograms with three sound values; these should be learned over time as the need arises. Like the biliterals they are usually accompanied by phonetic complements representing the second and third sound value:

Triliterals accompanied with **third** sound value only:

Triliterals accompanied with **second** and **third** sound value:

nfr 'good, happy, beautiful'

anx 'life, live'

Htp 'rest, at peace, satisfied'

Personal Pronouns (Continued)

4.3 Dependent Pronouns

The dependent pronouns are less attached to the previous word, but never stand alone at the beginning of a sentence.

wi 'I, me, my'

Tw 'you' masc.

Tn 'you' fem.

sw he, him, it'

sy 'she, her, it'

st 'she, her, it'

n(w) 'we, us'

Tn(w) 'you (plural)'

sn(w) 'they, them'

Note: sometimes the **T** sign is substituted with **t**.

Examples of use of the dependent pronouns:

hAb.k, wi send.you me 'you send me'

DA.n.f, sw ferry-across.of.he, him 'he ferried him across'

Vocabulary

isT 'lo!' **mk** 'behold' **nn** 'not'

ntt 'that' **nty** 'who, which'

m-bAH 'in the presence of'

Example sentences:

mk wi, m-bAH.k behold I, in the presence of.you
'behold, I am before you'

mk Tw, m bAk.i behold you, in-the-position-of servant.my
'behold, you are my servant'

nn s, m ib.i not it, in heart.my 'it was not in my heart'

sSm pn, nty wi, Xr.f state-of-affairs this, which I, under.it
'This state of affairs which I was under'

nfr.tw, Hna.i good.one/you, together-with.me 'you are good (happy) with me'

rdi.n.i, Hr Xt.i place.of.I, upon belly.my 'I placed myself, upon my belly'

Use of the word **st** 'she, her, it' which can also take on the meaning 'they, them, it':

st 'she, her, it, they, them'

Examples of use:

ann.sn(w) st turn-back.they it 'they turn it (themselves) around'

di.k, sDm st, sA.k cause.you, hear it, son.your 'you caused your son to hear it'

mk st, xft-Hr.k behold they, before/in-front face/sight.you 'Behold they (gifts, offerings) are before you'

bw nty st, im place which it, therein 'the place which it is therein ie the place where it is'

nfr st, r xt nbt beautiful it, more-than things all/any 'it is more beautiful than anything'

mk tw, Dd.tw behold one, says.one 'behold, one says'

4.4 Adjectives

Adjectives are words which describe a noun, such as in the phrase 'the small boat' the word '**small'** is the adjective and 'boat' is the noun (naming word). In sentences which involve adjectives they are written after the noun and the word endings of noun and adjective have the same gender, masculine or feminine, and the same number, singular, dual or plural. In Egyptian the phrase 'the **small** boat' is written as 'the boat **small'**.

Examples of use of **adjectives**:

sxr pn, bin plan this, **evil** 'this **evil** plan'

xt nbt, nfrt thing every, **good** 'every **good** thing'

Note: the adjective nfr 'good' is given the same feminine ending (**t**) following the feminine noun **xt** 'thing', noun and adjective are of the same gender. Although adjectives immediately follow after the noun, words like **nb** and **pn** and **suffix pronouns** precede the adjective:

sAt.f Srit daughter.his **little** 'His little daughter'

In Egyptian writing sometimes the **adjective** goes before its subject and does not change in gender or number:

nfr ib.i **happy** heart.my 'my happy heart'

bin sy **bad** she 'she is bad'

When used as **nouns**, adjectives such as in '**small**-boy, **beautiful**-woman', the adjective is followed by a determinative* which determine the meaning of the word:

Sri small + (small + *determinative for child) small-boy 'lad'

nfrt + (beautiful + *determinative for woman) 'beautiful woman'

nfrt + (*determinative for cow) 'beautiful cow'

Use of the dual ending **wy** to give an adjective more expression:

nfr.wy, pr pn beautiful.dual, house this Literally: doubly beautiful house this 'how beautiful is this house!'

Use of the preposition sign **r** 'more than' to express a comparison:

aSA st, r xt nbt many they, more-than thing any 'they were more than anything'

4.5 The Preposition 'n'

Examples of sentence syntax (sentence structure) using the preposition **n** 'to; for':

hAb.k, sS, n nb.k send.you scribe, **to** lord.your 'you send the scribe **to** your lord'

Dd.n, n.Tn speak.we, to.you (plural) 'we speak to you'

VOCABULARY 4

Learn and write out from memory the following words in hieroglyphs, with transliteration and meaning:

di give, place

di give, place

rdi give, place

rdi give, place

anx 'live, life'

Htp 'rest, go to rest, become at peace, set (of sun), peace (noun)'

aHa 'standup, arise'

xa 'appear, shine (of sun, gods or king)'

sxA 'remember'

nfr 'good, beautiful, happy'

bin 'bad, miserable'

Dw 'evil, sad'

aSA 'plentiful, rich, many'

, variation: **aA** 'great, large'

iqr 'excellent'

Sw 'empty, free'

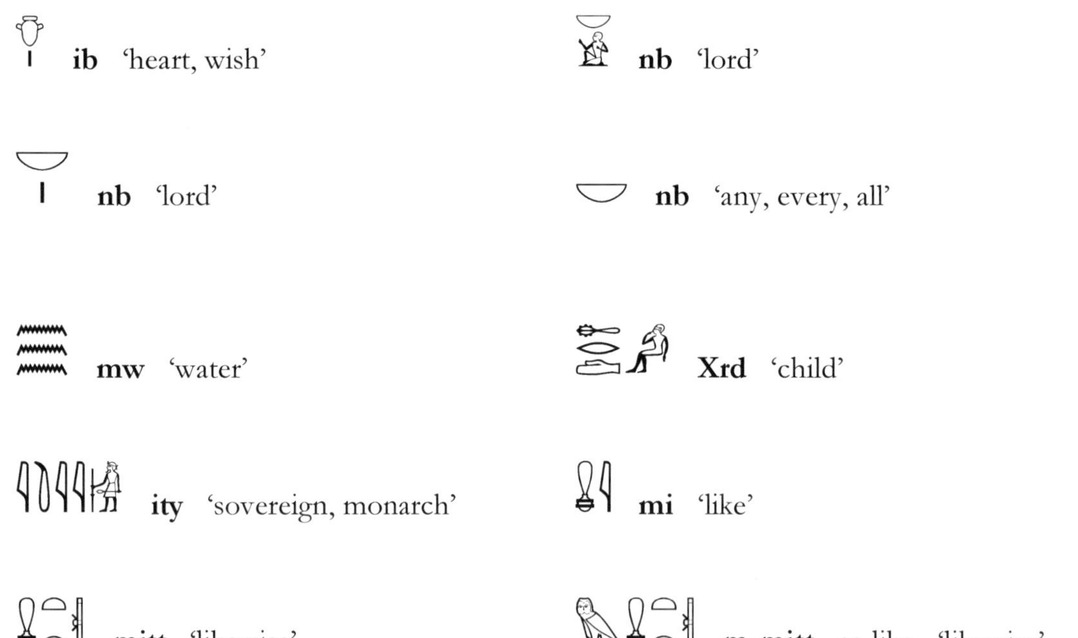

ib ‘heart, wish’

nb ‘lord’

nb ‘lord’

nb ‘any, every, all’

mw ‘water’

Xrd ‘child’

ity ‘sovereign, monarch’

mi ‘like’

mitt ‘likewise’

m-mitt as-like ‘likewise’

Study Note

Before proceeding use your notebook to practice the **biliteral signs** in lesson **3.1** and lesson **4.1**. Repetition is key: by repeatedly hand drawing the signs in a stylised short-hand form with thier transliteration you will gradually embed them in to your memory. Use up as many notebooks as you can when studying as repetition will also help you to develop your own hieroglyphic drawing technique.

EXERCISE 4

Transliterate and translate:

1.

2.

3.

4.

5.

6.

7.

LESSON 5

Independent Pronouns

5.1 Biliteral Signs

Study and learn the following biliteral signs:

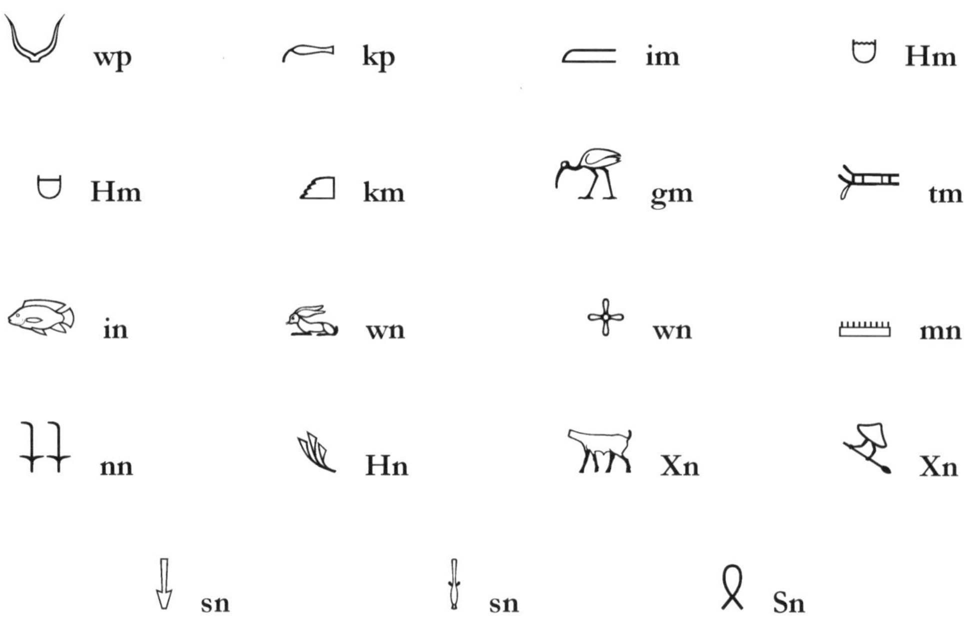

Remember: To aid memory the student should learn to draw the signs in a stylised short-hand form, carefully replicating the identifying shapes of the signs.

5.2 Peculiarities in Egyptian Writing

The following combination of signs should be learned as they are peculiar in avoiding general rules of writing and are therefore examples which conform by tradition to ways of spelling:

pr 'house' **mn** 'to be firm, remain' **Hm** 'male slave'

Hmt 'female slave' **Hm.f** 'His Majesty'

ib 'thirst' **xn** 'sentence, saying'

Htri 'pair of horses' **mAri** 'miserable'

nsw 'king' **nsw** 'king'

5.3 Abreviations

The following abbreviations (with full spellings) are commonest in monumental inscriptions, stereotyped phrases, formulae and titles:

anx wDA snb 'Life, Prosperity, Health'

anx 'life, live'

wDA 'prosperity'

snb 'health'

The above epiphet wish usually follows a person's name where it is preceded by the sign **rdi** 'to give':

(ra-ms-s-s) di anx wdA snb

'(Rameses) May he be given Life, Prosperity and Health'

mAa-xrw 'true (of) voice' **mAa-xrw** 'true (of) voice'

The above epiphet is usually added after the name of a deceased person and therefor identifies the person as 'deceased, venerated, justified, victorious'

wHm-anx 'reating life' **wHm-anx** 'reating life'

'Repeating life' is an example of another epiphet given to the deceased.

kA-nxt 'victorious bull' **kA-nxt** 'victorious bull'

'The Victorious Bull' was an attribute given to the pharaoh, from earliest times the pharaoh was depicted as a strong bull killing his enemies.

nsw-bit King-South-King-North 'King of Upper and Lower Egypt'

Literally, he who belongs to the sedge plant (**swt**) of Upper Egypt (South) and the bee of Lower Egypt (North Delta region).

HAty-a 'foremost in position' literally: 'front-hand'

imy-r(A) 'overseer' literally: 'he-who-is-in-mouth, in charge'

imy-r Hm-nTr 'overseer of the priests' literally: 'overseer of the god's slaves'

5.4 Graphic Transpositions

Some signs are deliberately put out of position or order by the scribe for various reasons: artistic symmetry, conserving space by maintaining a 'square group' of signs, or simply in honour of a god or king where their name is placed first, but spoken last. A small sign may be placed in front and under the breast of a bird even though the small sign should be read last, this is an example of maximizing space.

tw or **wt** according to the word in which it occurs

tA or **At** according to the word in which it occurs

wD the **w** is spoken first

wDA the **w** is spoken first

or  **AHt** 'field'

mr 'pyramid'

sbA 'star'

In the last example the star determinative should come last to end the word, but in this case for the economy of space it is put in the middle. The following examples demonstrate economy of space and abbreviation, each is followed by the full spelling:

Xry-Hb(t) 'lector priest'  literally: 'holder of the ritual book'

Xr-rdwy 'under the feet'

With regarding names of the kings or gods **nsw** 'king' and **nTr** 'god' were written before connected words even though they were spoke last:

sS-nsw (not **nsw-sS**) scribe-king 'Scribe of the king'

Hm-nTr (not **nTr-Hm**) servant-god 'servant of god, ie priest'

mi-ra (not **ra-mi**) 'like Ra'

mery-imn (not **imn-mry**) 'beloved of Amun'

5.5 Single Signs Concerning Motion

The mono phonogram **i** (two legs walking) is used with other phonograms for verbs concerning motion:

ii 'come'  **is** 'go'  **Sm** 'go'

ms 'bring, offer'  **sb (zb)** 'bring, conduct, pass'

iTi 'take, seize, carry off'  **ini** 'bring, fetch, remove'

sSm 'guide, lead'

5.6 Some Common Single Signs (Monograms):

tr in the word for 'season, time' — **tr** 'season, time'

rnp in the word for 'be young' — **rnpi** 'be young, vigorous'

m(i) in the word for 'neglectful' — **mhy** 'be neglectful'

mm in the word for 'not existing' — **tmm** 'not having been'

rsw in the word for 'south' — **rsy** 'south, southern' — **rsw** 'south wind'

SmAw 'Upper Egypt (the south)' — **Xrt-hrw** 'day-time' lit. 'under the sun'

aH 'palace' — **wDa** 'judge'

To conserve space in writing the hieroglyphic script, superfluous signs were omitted; therefore some words gained a standard spelling:

rmT (**m** omitted in writing) 'men, people'

Hnqt (**n** omitted in writing) 'beer'

Conversely to the above, some phonograms appear in a word but are not pronounced:

if (**w** omitted in reading) 'flesh, meat'

Ancient Egyptian hieroglyphic has many basic rules of writing, but just like any other language, whether by tradition, errors in reproduction, conservation of space or artistic symmetry, one can find examples of words, which seemingly ignore the rules and follow a standard form of depiction. This stresses the importance of learning the hieroglyphic writing system *by rote,* the student therefore should not concern or stress himself too much with the why?

More examples of such words where tradition of depiction overcomes basic rules:

ihi (not **iAhwiw**) 'foreign land'

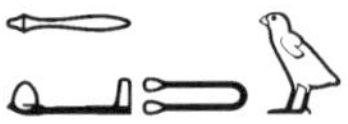

amT (not **aAmTw**) a man's name 'Ametj'

bw-nb 'everyone'

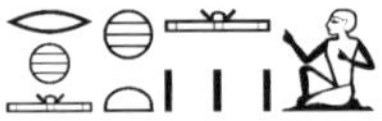

rx-xt a knower of things 'a wise man'

sS nxt 'the scribe Nakht'

5.7 Avoidance of Repetition

Where similar signs follow one another, one of the signs may be left out:

ini.n.f 'bring'

In the above example the repeating **n** can sometimes be omitted:

inf 'bring'

Personal Pronouns Continued

5.8 The Independent Pronouns

The independent personal pronouns almost always stand at the beginning of a sentence. Below is a list with their variations.

, , , **ink** 'I'

ntk 'you' masculine **ntT** 'you' feminine **ntt** 'you' feminine

ntf 'he, it' masculine **nts** 'she, it' feminine

inn(w) 'we' **inn(w)** 'we'

ntTn(w) 'you' plural **ntn(w)** 'you' plural

ntsn(w) 'they' plural **ntsn(w)** 'they' plural

Earlier forms of personal independent pronouns followed by their later forms:

Twt 'you' **twt** 'you'

swt 'he, she, it'

Examples of the use of the independent personal pronouns:

ink i.k I father.your 'I am your father'

ntf sA.s he son.hers 'he is her son'

Twt nb.i you lord.my 'you are my lord'

ink nfr good i 'I am good'

More examples of word order in sentences:

smi sS, sStA pn, n nb.f, m niwt.tn report scribe, secret this, to lord.his, in town this 'the scribe reports this secret to his lord in this town'

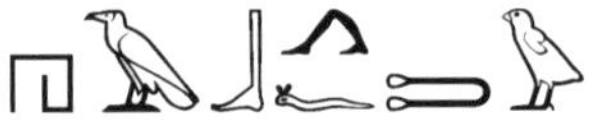

hAb.f, Tw send.he, you 'he sends you'

hAb Tw, sS, sends you, scribe 'the scribe sends you'

DA.Tn, sA.f ferries-across.you, son.his 'his son ferries you across' or 'you ferry across his son'

wSb.n.i, n.f, st answer.of.i, to.him, it 'I answered it to him'

in n.k, st, sS bring to.you, it, scribe 'the scribe brings it to you'

hAb.n, n.n(w), nb.n(w), nfr, Sat hr s send.of, to us, lord.our, good, dispatch concerning it 'our good lord has sent to us a dispatch about it'

twt.wy, n.s, st like.dual, to her, it 'how like to her it is'

nn n.k, st not of.you, it 'it is not of you' ie 'it does not belong to you'

iw n.k, hrw nfr is to.you, day good 'a good day is to you'

iw.f, n.i is.he, to.me 'he is mine'

5.9 Emphasis using Particles: *particles can provide emphasis and are not usually translated.*

Examples sentences using **ti** 'lo, behold, now', **grt** 'moreover, now', **rf** 'then, now' emphasis with wishes, commands, questions etc. and **Hm** 'assuredly, indeed':

Varaiations for **Hm**: , , **Hm** 'assuredly, indeed'

, **ti** 'lo, behold, now'

ir.n, grt, maHat(.i), r rd, n nTr aA made.of, now, in tomb(.my), at staircase, to god great 'now I made my tomb at the staircase of the great god'

s-Dd.i, rf, n.k, mtt iry cause-speak.i, indeed!, to you, like relating-to 'let me speak to you the like thereof'

ti sw, Hm, iy.f now it, indeed, come-forth.he 'now, indeed, he was returning'

5.10 Present to Past Tense: the sDm.n.f form of the verb

Unless otherwise indicated the student should translate sentences to present tense, however the insertion of the preposition **n** 'for, of, to' after a verb (doing word) group changes the sense to past tense:

The **sDm.f** present tense form:

sDm.f hears.he 'he hears'

With insertion of **n** becomes:

sDm.n.f heard.**of**.he 'he heard'

In Egyptian grammar this is called the **sDm.n.f** form of the verb. Example sentences expressing past tense:

sDm.n.i, xrw.f heard.of.i, voice.his 'I heard his voice'

sDm.n nTr, xrw heard.of god, voice 'the god heard the voice'

sDm.n st, ntr heard.of it, god 'the god heard it'

sDm.n.tw, xrw hear.of.one, voice 'one heard the voice' or 'the voice was heard'

pr.n.f go-out.of.he 'he went out'

hAb.n, n.k, nb.k send.of, to.you, lord.your 'your lord (has) sent to you'

ms.n.t(w).i born.of.one.i 'I was born'

ir.n.f, rnpwt aSAt, m Drt do.of.he, years many, in prison 'he has done many years in prison'

sxr.n.f, xftyw.f overthrow.of.he, enemies.his 'he has overthrown his enemies'

5.11 The use of the word iw 'behold!':

The use of the word **iw** 'is, are, behold' at the beginning of a sentence can give emphasis and importance to the following statements and can therefore be translated as 'behold!':

iw, in.n.i, Ddi behold, bring.of.i, Ddi 'behold! I have brought Djedi'

iw, wp.n.f, r.f, r.i behold, open.of.he, mouth.his, to.i 'behold, he opened, his mouth, to me'

5.12 Use of the word (r)di 'give, place' to mean 'cause, allow':

di.i, sDm.Tn(w) give.I, hear.you 'I give you to hear' ie 'I cause you to hear it.'

(r)di.t(w), iry.i, hrw m iaa give.one, do.i, day in Iaa 'I was allowed a day in Iaa'

VOCABULARY 5

Learn and write out from memory the following words in hieroglyphs, with transliteration and meaning:

in 'bring, fetch, remove'

wp 'open'

Sm 'go, walk'

gm 'find'

wab 'be pure, clean'

wab 'priest'

wSb 'answer' with **n** to persons

Hqr 'hungry, hunger'

ib 'thirst, thirsty'

mnx 'efficient, beneficent, excellent'

HAy 'naked'

kmt 'the Black Land, Egypt, ie the farmed fertile Nile Valley'

dSrt 'the Red Land, ie the barren sandy desert'

Xnw 'interior, inside'

sn 'brother'

snt 'sister'

Hmt 'woman, wife'

Hm 'male slave'

Hmt 'female slave'

nsw 'king of Upper Egypt, king'

nsw 'king of Upper Egypt, king'

nsw 'king of Upper Egypt, king'

nTr 'god'

nTr 'god'

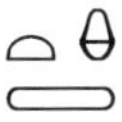

t 'bread

Hnqt 'beer'

Hbs 'clothes, clothing'

Tsm 'hound, dog'

sA 'back'

sA 'back'

m-sA 'at the back of, following after'

a 'hand, arm'

Study Note

Before proceeding use your notebook to practice the **personal pronoun signs** in lesson 4.3 and 5.8. Repetition is key: by repeatedly hand drawing the signs in a stylised short-hand form with thier transliteration and meaning you will gradually embed them in to your memory. Use up as many notebooks as you can when studying as repetition will also help you to develop your own hieroglyphic drawing technique.

EXERCISE 5

Transliterate and translate:

1\.

2\.

3\.

4\.

5\.

6\.

7\.

8\.

9\.

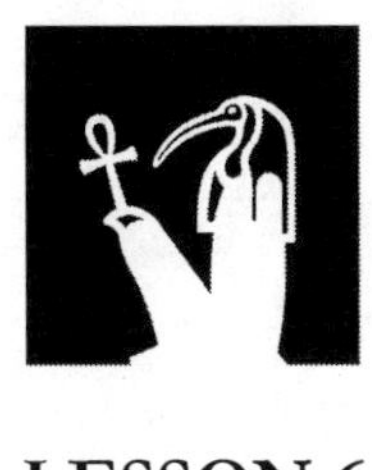

LESSON 6

Plural and Dual

6.1 Bilteral Signs (Continued)

Study and learn the following signs:

𓁹	**ir**	𓅨	**wr**	𓉐	**pr**	𓌻	**mr**	𓄣	**mr, Ab**	𓁷	**Hr**
𓌨	**Xr**	𓂦	**Dr**	𓄋	**bH**	𓄋	**pH**	𓍋	**mH**	𓅘	**nH**

6.2 Number Expressed in Word Ending Signs

There are three numbers to be expressed: singular (s.), plural (p.) and dual (d.): Nouns and adjectives have endings to express number. In English to express the singular we simply write: 'a book', to express the plural we add an 's' so the singular noun 'book' becomes 'books' and to express the dual we add the number: 'two books'. In Egyptian we must remember that there are masculine (m.) words, usually ending in **w**, even though most times this is omitted and feminine (f.) words ending in **t** and thus the number endings have masculine and feminine forms in the singular, plural and dual. The following should make this clear:

	Singular	Plural	Dual
Masculine	**-(w)**	**-w**	**-wy**
Feminine	**-t**	**-wt**	**-ty**

Singular ending signs: a single stroke: I

Plural ending signs: three strokes: I I I or ⁝ or ∘ ∘ ∘ or 𓏥

Dual ending signs: two strokes: \\ or II

sn 'brother' sing. masc. **snw** 'brothers' plur. masc.

snwy 'two brothers' dual masc.

snt 'sister' sing. fem. **snwt** 'sisters' plur. fem.

snty 'two sisters' dual fem.

The plural of **nsw** 'king' is written:

nswyw 'kings'

In older forms of writing the number was expressed by depicting the singular ideogram, twice for the dual and thrice for the plural:

pr 'house' **prw** 'houses' **prwy** 'two houses'

irt 'eye' **irty** 'two eyes'

More archaic examples of words expressing number by repeating ideograms and determinatives:

srw 'officials' **nhwt** 'trees'

txnwy 'two obelisks' **aty** 'two limbs'

nTrw 'gods **nTrwy** 'two gods'

rn 'name' **rnw** 'names'

HkA 'magic spell' **hHkAw** 'magics spells'

By the end of the Old Kingdom to express the plural a determinative of three strokes (**w**) or three dots was used, this replaced repeating the determinative three times:

snw 'brothers'

nTrw 'gods'

prw 'houses'

nfrw 'beautiful'

.they '.they'

rxyt 'people, subjects'

aSA 'many'

Likewise, to express the dual a determinative of two strokes (**y**) was originally used to replace repeating the determinative twice. Later the two strokes become adopted for the letter **y**.

Examples of number for study where sometimes the plural and dual endings are omitted in one of the words:

Apdw DdA(w) birds fat 'fat birds'

kAw wADw oxen sturdy 'sturdy oxen'

awy.i hands-dual.my 'my hands'

rdwy feet-dual.my 'my feet'

awy.fy hands-dual.his 'his two hands'

spty.ky lips-dual.your 'your two lips'

mnty.sy two-thighs.her 'her two thighs'

gs(wy).fy two-sides.his 'his two sides'

pH(wy).fy end.its 'its end'

sn-nw.fy second.his 'his second'

The following abstract words are spelt and written like plurals and duals:

nfrw thrice beautiful 'beauty'

mnw 'memorial, monument'

hAw 'neighbourhood, time'

xAwy 'night'

niwty 'belonging to a town'

niwty 'belonging to a town'

pHty 'strength' ie doubly strong

pHty 'strength'

Hnty 'period, end'

irp 'wine'

nbw 'gold'

mw 'water'

mnmnt 'herd'

Xnyt 'sailors'

rmT 'man' singular

rmT 'men' plural collective

rmT nbt man all 'all men'

6.3 Adjectives (Describing Words) ending in (y)

In English we can often change the meaning of a word by adding an ending: 'south' can be come 'southern' and 'north' can become 'northern', simply by adding the ending '-ern'. In Egyptian adding the ending (-y) can change a noun (naming word, such as 'book') and a preposition (a word that becomes before an object in a sentence and describes its state, such as 'to' or 'on') into an adjective. The following examples demonstrate:

Nouns into adjectives:

rsw 'south-wind'

rs-y 'southern'

mHyt 'north wind'

mHyty 'northern'

Note: in the first example the determinative for 'wind', the sail, is dropped and the two stokes for 'y' is added followed by the determinative for 'land'.

Prepositions into adjectives:

r 'to' **ir** 'to' **iry** 'relating to, connected with'

Further examples of words ending with (-y) and their transformations for study:

xft 'before, opposite' **xftyw** 'opponents, enemies'

Note: the use of the **tyw** bird, a sound sign, to give the **ty** and the **w** plural ending:

Gardiner G4 **tyw** the **tyw** bird, a long legged buzzard, often indistinguishable from:

Gardiner G1 **A** a vulture

Further transformation examples for study of words ending in **y**:

Hr 'upon' **Hry** 'above'

The above example transformation uses the two stroke sign for **y** and the determinative for sky.

m 'in' **imy** '(who is) in'

Important examples of abbreviations, derivations and transformations:

imy-r 'overseer' Literally: 'one who is in the mouth'

nTr-niwty god-town 'local god' **Axty** 'Horus of the (Two) Horizon(s)'

Hr-StA 'he who is over the secret'

imt.f that-being-in-it 'what is in it' **mity** 'like, equal'

mity.f equal.his 'his equal'

tp 'upon' preposition **tp** 'head, chief, beginning of (year, season, morning'

tpy 'foremost, chief, first, being upon'

inpw tpy, Dw.f Anubis upon, mountain.his 'Anubis upon his mountain'

imt.sn(w), HAt being-in.their, front 'their originals'

iry nb, sSm relating-to every, business 'everyone relating to a business'

n(y) wi, ra belonging-to I, Ra 'I belong to Ra'

sxt 'marsh land, country' **sxty** 'peasant, fowler, one belonging to the country'

imntt 'west' **imnty** 'western'

Xr 'under' **Xrt-nTr** under-god 'necropolis'

Hr(y)w Sa those-upon sand 'the Bedawin'

VOCABULARY 6

Learn and write out from memory the following words in hieroglyphs, with transliteration and meaning:

ir 'make, do'

pr 'go forth, go up'

pH 'reach, arrive, attack'

mr 'love, wish'

mH 'fill, be full'

HAq 'capture, take as plunder'

dbH 'ask for, beg'

imnty 'western'

iAbty 'eastern'

wr 'great, important, much'

kAS 'Ethiopia, the Cush of the Bible'

irtt 'milk'

mnw 'monument'

mnmnt 'cattle'

rmT 'man'

rmTt 'people'

rd 'foot'

nHH 'eternity'

tAS 'boundary'

mr 'pyramid'

it 'barley, corn'

Xt 'body'

xAst 'hill country, (foreign) country'

Xr 'under, carrying, holding'

Study Note

Before proceeding use your notebook to practice the **adjective signs** in lesson **4.2** and **6.3**. Repetition is key: by repeatedly hand drawing the signs in a stylised short-hand form with thier meaning you will gradually embed them in to your memory. Use up as many notebooks as you can when studying as repetition will also help you to develop your own hieroglyphic drawing technique.

EXERCISE 6

Transliterate and translate:

1.

2.

3.

4.

5.

6.

7.

8.

9.

10.

LESSON 7

Noun and Pronoun Syntax

7.1 Biliteral Signs (Continued)

Study and learn the following signs:

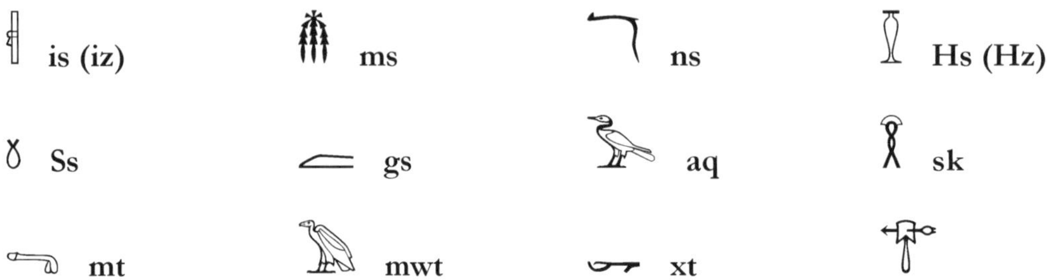

7.2 Syntax of Sentences

Study the following examples taking note of literal translation into full English translation:

ir.n, wi, ary.i, m rxxy make.of, I, reed-pen.my, in-the-position-of/as known-one 'My pen made me known'

rid.n.f, wi m, Hr niwt.f made.of.he, I in-the-position-of, over town.his he made me as over his town 'He placed me as chief over his town'

rdi.n.f, sw, r rpat HAty-a place.of.he, him, to prince local-mayor 'He placed him as a prince and local ruler'

Vocabulary:

sbA 'teach' **imy-r pr** overseer house 'overseer of the house'

Syntax Examples:

nb-imAx all-venerated-state 'possessor/lord of veneration' **xrt** 'state, condition'

rx xrt-ib, nb.f know state-heart, lord.his 'knowing the desire of his lord'

imy-r sxtyw mnx overseer fowlers efficient 'efficient overseer of fowlers'

7.3 Honorific Transposition

Examples of honorific transposition: where the name of the god or king is placed first but spoken last:

signs	graphic	written	literal	translation
	nTr-Hm	**Hm-nTr**	servant of god	'priest'
	nTr-Hwt	**Hwt-nTr**	house-god	'temple'
	nsw-pr	**pr-nsw**	house-king	'palace'
	nsw-sA	**sA-nsw**	son-king	'prince'

7.4 Syntax expressing 'son of' filiation:

After the 12 th Dynasty

iaH-ms, sA (n) ibAn Iahmose, son (of) Ibn 'Iahmose, son of Ibaen'

In the 12th Dynasty and earlier the inverse was used:

nri sA, Xnm-Htp sA, Xnm-Htp Nery's son, Khenemhotep's son, Khenemhotep 'Khenemhotep, son of Khenemhotep, son of Nery'

7.5 The word (ny) 'belonging to' and its derivatives:

Masculine forms:

ny 'belonging to' masc. sing. **nw** 'belonging to' masc. plur.

nwy 'belonging to' masc. dual

Feminine forms:

nt 'belonging to' fem. sing. **nywt** 'belonging to' fem. plur.

nty 'belonging to' fem. dual

Exmples of use:

nsw, n kmt king, belonging-to Egypt 'King of Egypt'

niwt, nt nHH city, belonging-to eternity 'the city of eternity'

wrw, nw AbDw great-ones, of Abydos 'Great Ones of Abydos'

aAw, n sxty pn donkeys, of peasant this 'the donkeys of this peasant'

Hmwt, nt srw wives, of chiefs 'the wives of the chiefs'

inw nb, nfr, n sxt gifts-tribute all, good, of country 'all good produce of the country'

imyw-r.k, n rwyt overseers.your, of portal (gateway, place of judgement) 'your overseers of the portal'

sDAwt im.f, nt pr-HD treasure therein.it, of house-white (treasury) 'the valuables within it belonging to the treasury'

7.6 The Expressive Vocatives: listen, behold, O! Ah! Ho!

Emphasis is usually expressed at the start of a sentence:

The use of 'behold, O, ha, ho' in the calling or addressing a person in a sentence:

mk 'behold' **i** 'O!' **i** 'O!'

hA 'Ha!, Ho!' **hA** 'Ha!, Ho!'

Examples expressing the vocative:

Hsw, Hs(y) tw, Hry-S.f praise/favour, praised-one one, Hery-sh-ef 'O praised one, Heryeshef* praises you'

*Hery-sh-ef: 'He who is upon the lake'. Greek: Arsaphes, the ram god of Heracleopolis)

sDm rk, n.i, HAty-a listen you!, to.me, **prince** 'Listen to me, O Prince'

mk, wi r nHm, aA.k, sxty, Hr wnm.f, Sma.i

behold!, I to take-away, donkey.your, because eat.it, corn.my
'Behold, I will take away your donkey, peasant, because it is eating my corn'

i, nb snD O!, lord fear 'O!, lord of fear'

i, anxw O!, living-ones 'O!, living ones'

hA!, sS, nbsny ha!, scribe, nbsny 'Ha! Scribe, Nebseny'

Sms ib.k, tr, n wnn.k follow heart.your, time of exist.you
'follow your heart as long as you live'

iw, s-anx.n.(i), iw-mi-itrw, rnpwt qsnt
behold, made-to-live.of.(i), Iw-mi-itrw (island-like-river-town), years painful/difficult 'Behold, I made live (nourished), the city of Imiotru, in troubled years'

7.7 Time and Number

Some important vocabulary involving time and number:

HAt-sp 'regnal year, reigning year of the king' **Dt** 'eternity'

ra-nb day-every 'every day' **mD** 10 'the number ten'

sp-10 'ten times'

Hat-sp, wDA Hm.f regnal-year 12, go/proceed majesty.his 'in year 12 (of his rein), His Majesty proceeded'

7.8 Noun syntax examples:

spd Hr sharp (of) face 'clever'

nTr.Tn(w), bnr mrwt god.your, sweet love 'your god, sweet of love'

rx.n.f, Ax.i, n.f, ib know.of.he, beneficent.i, to.his, heart 'he knew I was beneficent to him in heart'

7.8 Headings, lists comments and phrases etc in hieroglyphic texts:

Title introducing a prescription:

kt pXrt another remedy 'another remedy'

Item in a list of goods:

wrs-1 head-rest 1 'one head-rest'

Written over a picture of a brewer:

afty nxt brewer Nakhet 'the brewer, Nakhet'

Comment accompanying a spell:

sSr mAa manner-of-action true/real 'a real remedy'

kt Hswt, iryt n.i another favour, make to.me 'Another favour that was done to me'

'If the workmen are here waiting for their pay, then...

bw nb nfr place/position all good 'all is well and good' or 'Everyone is good'

Statement accompanying the cartouche name of a king:

ar nTr, r Axt.f, nsw bit (ra-stp-ib) ascend god, to tomb.his, king-upper-lower-Egypt (Ra-setep-ib) 'The god ascended to his tomb (horizon), the king of Upper and Lower Egypt, Se-hetep-ib-ra'

m-xmt.f, nTr pf mnx without.him, god that excellent 'without him, that excellent god'

Hna, aS xAy(t) wrt together-with, pine table-of-offerings great 'together with the great alter of cedar'

Hnqt ds-2 beer beer-measure-2 'two jugs of beer'

tA-wr, AbDw land-great (Thinite-Nome-of Abydos), Abydos 'Abydos, in the Thinite Nome'

7.9 Juxtaposition of nouns for the word 'and'

The absence of the word '**and**' in Egyptian is solved by placing two words together, thus the two words, **s st**, 'man' 'woman' becomes 'man and woman':

s st man woman 'man **and** woman'

gm.n.i, dAbw iArrt, im find.of.i, figs grapes, there 'I found figs **and** grapes there'

tAS.f, rsy mHty boundary.it, southern northern 'its southern **and** northern boundary'

iAwt.Tn, prw.Tn offices.your, houses.your 'your offices **and** your houses'

xt.i nbt, m SA, m niwt property.my all, in country, in town 'all my property in country **and** in town'

Closely connected words may be connected with **Hr** 'upon' or else **Hna** 'together with':

Da Hr Hyt wind **upon** rain 'wind **and** rain'

msw.i, Hna, senw.i children.my, **together-with**, brothers.my 'my children **and** my brothers'

Note: the word 'or' as like the word 'and' may not be expressed:

Tsw nb, HAty-a nb commander any, prince any 'Any commander or any prince'

In some cases the phrase **r-pw** is used to express the word 'or' and is placed at the end of the alternatives:

r 'to, at, concerning, more than, from, so that, until, according as'

pw 'this, who? what? whichever' **r-pw** 'or'

m nb, m sn, m xnms,r- pw as lord, as brother, as friend, or (to-whichever) 'As lord, as brother, **or** as friend'

7.10 Noun Gender

Names of foreign countries and towns usually have a feminine ending (**t**):

kAS Xst Cush vile 'the vile Cush (Ethiopia)'

The word **xt** 'things, property' is treated as feminine, but when expressed as 'something, anything' it is treated as masculine:

xt mr something painful 'Something painful'

Some words like **xt** 'wood, tree' is not treated as feminine, while **Xt** 'body' can be treated as masculine or feminine:

xt 'tree, wood' **Xt** 'body, belly'

xt nDm wood sweet 'sweet (smelling) wood'

xt qA tree high 'a high tree'

VOCABULARY 7

Learn and write out from memory the following words in hieroglyphs, with transliteration and meaning:

aq 'enter'

wsTn 'stride'

wstn 'stride'

nxt 'be mighty, victorious, mighty'

sns 'worship'

Ssp 'receive, take'

Ssp 'receive, take'

st 'place'

xrw 'voice, sound'

xrw 'voice, sound'

xrw 'voice, sound'

Awt 'oblations, offerings'

wDHw 'table of offerings'

wDHw 'table of offerings'

isft 'evil, wrong-doing'

isft 'evil, wrong-doing'

Sbw ‘food’

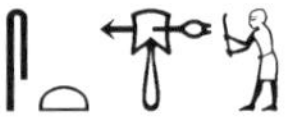

st ‘shoot, throw, pour’

mwt ‘mother’

ms ‘child’

sxAw ‘remembrance, memory’

mAa ‘true, real, just’

sbA ‘door’

sbA ‘door’

Dt ‘eternity, everlasting’

Hst ‘praise, favour’

dwA ‘adore, worship’

ms ‘child’

Dw ‘mountain’

sxAw ‘remembrance, memory’

mAa ‘true, real, just’

sbA ‘door’

dwAt ‘underworld’

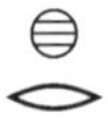

xr ‘with, before, (speak) to’

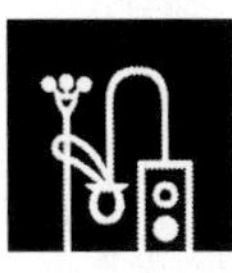

EXERCISE 7

a) Study the following funerary wishes from a Theban noble's tomb, Dynasty 18:

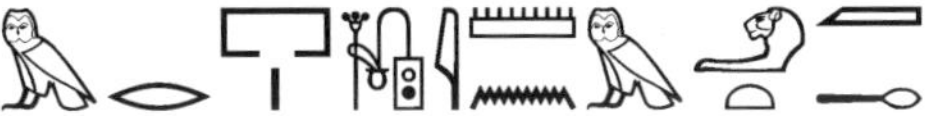

imy-r pr, sS imn-m-HAt, mAa xrw
overseer house, scribe Imenemhat, true-voice

'Overseer of the House (Steward), Scribe Amenemhet, True of Voice (Justified).'

aq.k pr.k, m imnt
enter.you, go-forth.you, from west

'May you enter and go forth from the West.'

wstn.k, Hr sbA, n dwAt
stride.you, through door, of underworld

'May you stride through the door of the underworld.'

dwA.k ra, wbn.f, m Dw
adore.you Ra, rises.he, in mountain

'May you adore Ra when he rises in the mountain.'

sns.k, sw, Htp.f, m Axt

worship.you, him, set/rest.he, in horizon

'May you worship him when he sets in the horizon.'

Ssp.k, Awt, Htp.k

receive.you, oblations, satisfied.you

'May you receive oblations and be satisfied.'

Hr Sbw, Hr wdHw, n nb Dt

because-of food, upon alter, of lord eternity

'Because of the food upon the alter of the lord (of) eternity'

Note: the 'lord of eternity' was Osiris the god of the underworld.

Study Note

Before proceeding use your notebook to practice the alphabetic sound signs in lesson 1 and the determinative signs in lesson 2. This will help to refresh your knowledge and prepare you for the next exercise.

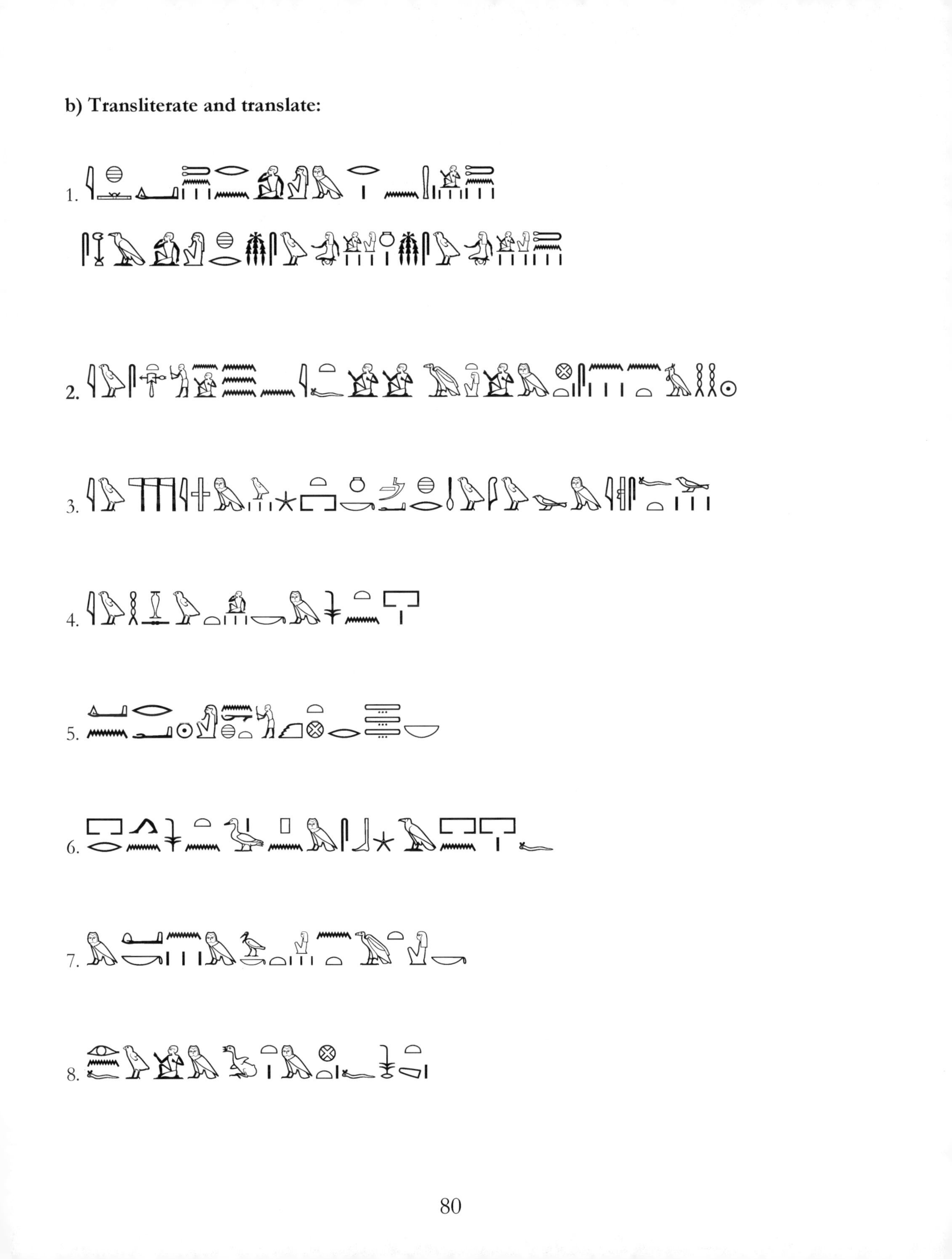

b) Transliterate and translate:

1.

2.

3.

4.

5.

6.

7.

8.

LESSON 7 - STUDY

The Titulary and Other Designations of the King

7.1 Names and Titles of Kheper-ka-ra

The pharaoh was given five great names (**rn-wr**) in the day of his coronation as king:

rn-wr name-great 'geat name'

The following example is the full titulary of Sesostris I (Dynasty 12):

Hr anx mswt, nbty anx mswt, Hr-nwbw-anx-mswt
Horus life birth, Two-Ladies life birth, Horus gold life birth

'Horus Life of Births, Two-Ladies Life of Births, Horus of Gold Life of Births'

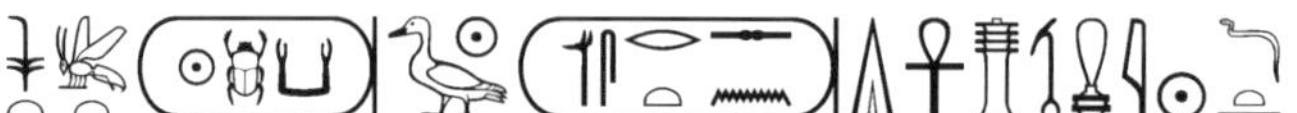

n-sw-bit (xpr-kA-ra) sA-ra (sn-wsrt) di, anx Dd wAs, mi ra, Dt
King-South-North (Kheper-ka-ra) son-Ra (Sen-wasret) given, life stability power, like ra, eternity

'King of Upper and Lower Egypt,Kheper-ka-ra, Son of Ra Senwasret,
may he be given, life, stability and power, like Ra, forever'

The Son of Ra name: Kheper-ka-ra:
Literally translates as: come-into-existence soul (of) Ra: 'The soul of Ra comes into being'.

The Nsw Bit name: Sen-wasret:
Literally translates as: man of Wasret (goddess): 'Man of the goddess Wasret.'

7.2 The Titulary of Tuthmoses III (Dynasty 18):

Hr ka nxt, xa m wAst, nbty, wAH nsyt, ra mi, m pt

Horus bull strong, shine-appear in Waset, Two-Ladies, enduring kingship, Ra like, in heaven

'Horus, strong bull appearing in Thebes, Two Ladies, enduring of kingship, like Ra in heaven'

sxm Hr pHty Dsr kaw, n-sw-bit (mn-xpr-ra), zA-ra (ms-DHwty, nfr-xpr), Ht-Hr, nbt mfkAt, mry

power Horus-Golden, strength double, sacred crowns, king S.N. (Men-kheper-Ra), son-Ra (Mes- Djhwty, Nefer-kheper), Hathor, lady-turquoise, beloved

'Golden Horus, Powerful of Strength, Holy of Crowns, King of Upper and Lower Egypt, Men-kheper-ra, Son of Ra, Mes-Djhwty, Nefer-kheper, Beloved of Hathor, Lady of the Turquoise'

The nsw-bit name: **Men-kheper-ra:**
Literally translates as: 'Established Created Form of Ra'

The Son of Ra name: **Djhwty-mes, Nefer-kheper:**
Literally translates as: 'Thoth is born, Beautiful of Created Form.'

7.3 The Five Royal Names

The Egyptian kings were distinguished by five royal names:

1. The Horus Name

In the Horus name the king is associates himself with the falcon god Horus. This name is frequently placed within a rectangular frame called the serekh which was mounted by a sign for the god Horus:

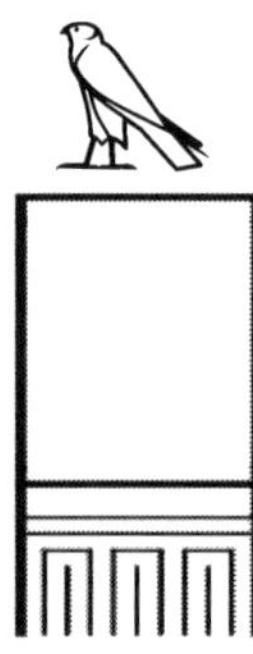

srx 'serekh'

At the base of the serekh is what appears to be a tomb false door or the palace facade. The open rectangle at the top where the name was inscribed may represent the actual tomb or the palace courtyard.

2. The Nebty Name

In the Nebty 'Two Ladies' name the king associates himself the two goddesses of ancient Egypt, representing the unity of Upper and Lower Egypt:

nxbt 'Nekhbet' The vulture goddess of Upper Egypt

wADt 'Wadjet' The cobra goddess of Lower Egypt.

nbty 'Two Ladies'

3. The Golden Horus Name

In the Golden Horus name: the king associates himself with a falcon of gold. The Golden Horus name is depicted with a falcon seated over the sign for gold:

Hr 'Horus' **nbw** 'gold' **Hr nbw** 'Horus of Gold'

4. The Nesew Bit (Throne) name

The Nesew Bit name gives the title of 'King of Upper and Lower Egypt,' literally: 'he of the Sedge plant of the South and the Bee of the North delta region.'

swt 'the flowering scirpus reed plant'

bit 'bee' bity 'king'

nsw bit 'king of upper and lower Egypt'

5. The Son of Ra Name

The Son of Ra name is the name that the king was known before ascension to the throne. It is likened to a birth or family name.

Both the Nesew Bit (Throne) name and the Sa Ra name are usually enclosed within a cartouche.
To introduce the king's name the phrase **Hm-n** 'the majesty of' was often used:

Hat-sp 19, xr Hm-n, nTr nfr regnal-year 19, under majesty-of, god good 'Regnal year 19 under the majesty of the good god'

nb-tAwy (n-mAat-ra) sA-ra (imn-m-Hat) lord-two-lands (n-mat-Ra) son-ra (Amen-em-hat) 'Lord of the Two Lands (Ne-mat-ra) Son of Ra (Amen-em-hat)'

As speaker the king often referred to himself as Hm.i 'My Majesty':

Hm.i majesty.my 'my Majesty' **Hm.i** majesty.my 'my Majesty'

Hm.k majesty.your 'your Majesty' **Hm.k** majesty.your 'your Majesty'

Hm.f majesty.his 'his Majesty' **Hm.f** majesty.his 'his Majesty'

m Hm stp-sA in majesty of palace 'in the majesty of the palace'

7.4 Names referring to the king:

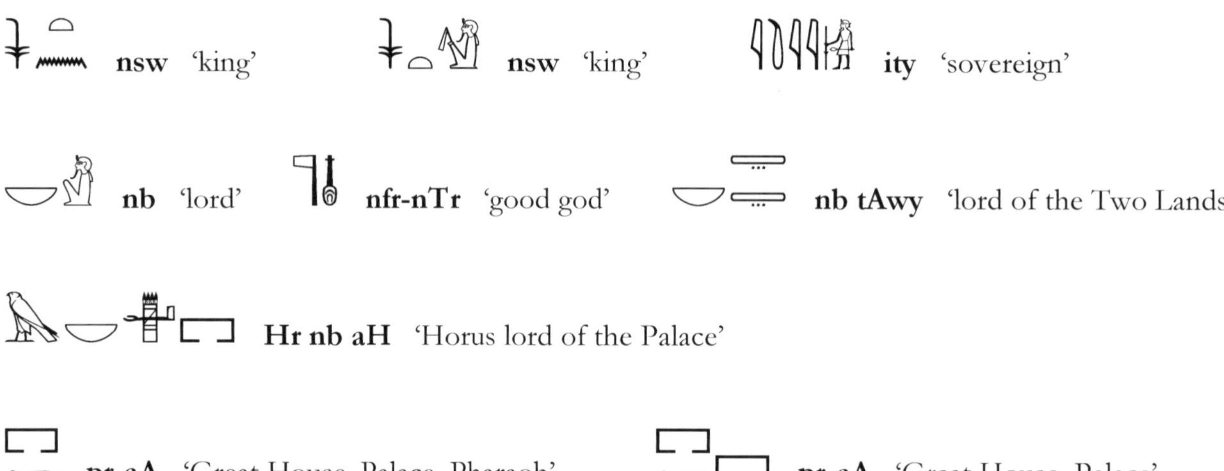

nsw 'king' **nsw** 'king' **ity** 'sovereign'

nb 'lord' **nfr-nTr** 'good god' **nb tAwy** 'lord of the Two Lands'

Hr nb aH 'Horus lord of the Palace'

pr-aA 'Great House, Palace, Pharaoh' **pr-aA** 'Great House, Palace'

Note: the earliest possible reference to **pr-aA** 'Great House' as referring to the king himself (**Pharaoh**) was in a letter to Akhenaten during the 18th Dynasty:

aA-pr anx wDA snb nd great-house life prosperity health, lord 'Pharaoh, life, health and prosperity, the lord'

LESSON 8

Syntax of Adjectives

8.1 Biliteral Signs (continued)

Sd qd qd aD wD wD

nD HD

8.2 Syntax of Adjectives

Study the following sentences taking note of the use of the **adjectives** (describing words). Note the position of the adjective and the word it describes in the hieroglyphic, transliteration and translation.

swt.f, nt r-qrrt, Dsrt, imt sAwt
places.his, of Rokereret, **holy**, therein Sawt (Siut) 'his **holy** places of Rokereret, which are in Siut'

wa, im nb one/alone, therein all 'Each one thereof'

t-HD.sn(w) bread-**white**.their 'their **white** bread'

gs-Hry.sn side-**upper**.their 'their **upper** side'

Hwrw n rxty **wretched** of washerman 'a **wretched** washerman'

a n, Tbwt n HD item/piece of, sandals of white 'a pair of **white** sandals'

sS iqr, n Dbaw.f scribe excellent, of fingers.his 'a scribe excellent with his fingers'

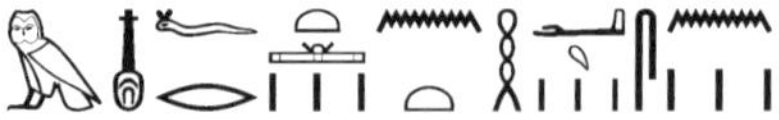

m nfrwt, nt Haw.sn(w) as beautiful, of body-members.their 'who are beautiful of body'

8.3 Sentences with expressive adjectives:

ir ib qn, m st, qsnt, sn-nw pw, n nb.f as-to heart strong, in place, difficult, second this, of lord.it 'as to a brave heart in the evil place, it is the equal of its lord'

wr twA, n sfw, r nxt great claim/appeal, of gentle/mild-man, to strong 'greater is the claim of the gentle (man), than that of the strong'

Dd.i, wrt say.I, great 'I speak great' ie 'I say great things'

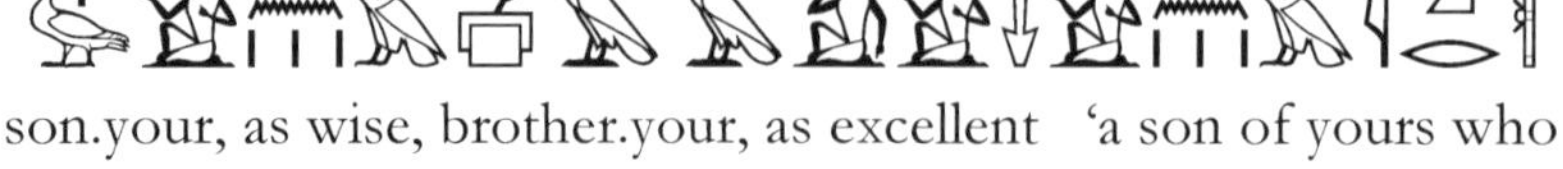

sA.tn(w), m sAA, sn.tn(w), m iqr son.your, as wise, brother.your, as excellent 'a son of yours who is wise, a brother of yours who is excellent'

iry.i, m wrt do.I, as great 'I will do (something) which is great'

iw, anxw tpyw-tA, m nTr-Hmw, nTr-Hmwt, nw r-pr, pn O, living upon-earth, as god-man-servants, god-maid-servants, of temple, this 'O you living upon the earth, such are as priests and priestesses of this temple'

8.4 Sentences expressing comparison and superlative statements:

The preposition **r** is often used: 'to, at, more than'.

wr n wrw great of great-ones 'greatest of the great ones'

ink, wr wrw, m tA, r Dr.f I-am, great greats, in land, to end.its 'I was greatest of the greats in the entire land'

wr imy saHw great therein nobles 'greatest of the nobles'

zA.f, smsw.f son.his, eldest.his 'his son, his eldest'

StA wrt secret/difficult great 'very difficult'

r xt nbt to/more-than thing any 'more than anything'

wa iqr one/alone excellent 'uniquely excellent'

8.5 Equivalents of English adjectives:

The words for 'other':

ky 'other' masc. sing. — **kt** 'other' fem. sing.

kywy 'other' masc. plur. — **kt** 'other' fem. plur.

Examples of use:

kt pXrt 'another remedy'

ky sp 'another time'

kywy nsyw 'other kings'

kt xt 'other things'

The expressions of **wa** 'one' and **ky** 'other':

iw, wAt.f, wat Xr mw, kt Xr it behold, way/road/side.it, one/alone under water, other under corn 'Behold, its one side was under water, the other under corn'

Hpt.n, ky ky embrace.of, other other 'one embraced the other'

wa Dd.f, xft, sn-nw.f one says.he/it, in-front-of, second.his 'One said, to, the other'

rdi.n, wi xAst, n xAst give.of, I land, of land 'land gave me to land'

Examples of the use of **HH** 'million' and **nhy** 'a little' for 'many, a few, a little':

HH 'a great number, a million' **nhy** 'a little'

Examples:

HH n sp great-number of times 'many times'

nhy n rmT a-little of men 'a few men'

nhy n HmAt a-little of salt 'a little salt'

Phrases using **Dr** and the like for the meanings 'entire, complete, whole':

r Dr.f to end.it 'to its end'

tA pn, r Dr.f land this, to end.its 'this entire land'

mSa r Dr.f army to end.its 'the entire army'

dr.n.f, s(y), r Dr.s subdue.of he, it, to end.it 'he subdued the whole of it'

nn n xt, r Dr these of things, to end entirety of these things 'All of these things'

nb-r-Dr lord-to-end 'lord of the Universe' or 'lord of All'

Nb-r-Dr was a title given to the sun god or king, likewise, **Nbt-r-Dr** 'Lady of the Universe' was a title given to the queen.

Use of **mi-qd.f** like-form.its 'like its form':

wnwt nTr-Hwt, mi-qd.s priestly-duties/priesthood temple, like-its-form 'the entire priesthood of the temple'

Use of **r-Aw.f** to length.it 'according to its length':

hrw, r Aw.f day, to its length 'The entire (whole) day'

tA Xnyt, r Aw.s the-navy, to length.it 'the entire navy'

nn, r Aw, n rnpwt these, to end, of years 'all of these years'

Phrases used for the words **Tnw, tnw** 'each, every' of time:

Tnw 'number, every'

tnw 'number, every'

r Tnw rnpwt to every years 'every year'

tnw dwAw every morning 'every morning'

The use of **s** 'man' for the words 'someone, anyone' and with a negative word for 'no one':

ir, xA.k, s(w) if, examine(a patient).you, man 'if you examine someone'

nn wn ib, n s(w) not exist heart, of man 'not one has a heart'

Phrases using **nb** 'any' and the like for phrases with the meaning 'everyone, anyone, every-place, each one, each, every thing, anything':

s nb man every 'everyone'

bw nb(w) place every 'every place'

Hr nb face every 'every face'

wa nb sole-one every 'everyone'

xt nbt things any/all 'all things, anything'

xt things 'something, anything'

NEGATION

8.6 The Syntax of Sentences and Phrases using Negation

The commonest use in Egyptian for negation is the use of the negativie word **nn** or **n** 'no, not':

nn 'not' **n** 'not'

The sign used for **nn** (Kemet Scribe Sign List & Gardiner's Sign List D35) is a pair of arms in opposition (negation):

There are variants of the use of the word **nn**:

nn 'not' **nn** 'not'

Examples:

n sDm.f not hear.he 'he did not hear' past tense

nn sDm.f not hear.he 'he will not hear' future tense

Note: the above **n sDm.f** form of the verb negatation expresses past tense, while the **nn sDm.f** form expresses future tense.

Example sentences showing the syntax of negation:

n, ir.(i) xt, n Srr nb, ir.n.(i), xt n HAty-a not, do.I things, for small-man any, done.I things for prince 'I did not do things for any small man, I did things for the prince'

ii.n.i, n xpr nhw, m mSa.i come.of.I, not become/happened loss, in army.my 'I returned, there had not occurred (happened) loss in my army'

nn wTs.f, dSrt not lift/carry/wear.he, red-crown 'he shall not wear the red crown' (Here the future tense is expressed by the word **nn)**

n mdw.n.f not speak.of.he/it 'he/it does not speak' (here the **n sDm.n.f** form has present meaning as is often the case)

Note: when the student is unclear during translation concerning past, present or future tense, it is advised to translate into present tense.

anw pw, n redi.n.f, sA.f one-who-always-returns this, not give.of.he, back.his 'This one who always returns, does not turn (give) his back'

Note: again, in the sentence where **n sDm.nf** is used the present tense is expressed, but in these cases the student should not over concern themselves with the tense of the verbal sentence, but rather concentrate on expressing the negation of the verb: 'He does not hear' 'he will not hear' 'he did not hear.' All express negation.

n, sqd.n, dpt, Hr.f not, sail.of, boat, upon.it 'no boat sailed upon it'

n, pr.n.f not, come-out.of.it 'It will not (never) come out'

The above expression of the word 'never' is more clearly expressed by the use of the phrase **n sp**:

n zp not happen 'it did not happen, never'

n sp, iry.i, xt nbt Dwi, r rmT nb not happen, do.I, thing evil any, to people any 'never did I anything evil against any people'

n sp, ir.t(w) mtt, Dr pAt tA not happen, do.one like, end ancient-time earth never, done.one the like, to the entire ancient time of earth 'Never had the like been done, since the primeval age of the earth'

8.7 To express existence, 'to exist, to be' syntax:

Syntax of sentences to express the words and meaning of 'existence, to exist' is done by use of the word **wnn** 'exist, be':

wnn 'exist, be, **when'**

With regard to tense (time) there are two forms commonly used:

wnn.f exist.he 'he will exist' **future** tense or to a time expressed

wn.f exists.he 'he exists' **past** tense or no reference to time

wnn pt, wnn.T, xr.i exist heaven, exist.you, with.me 'as long as heavens exists, you shall exist with me'

HD.n.i, wn hrw go-out.of.I, exists (when) day 'I set out when it was day'

iw wn behold/is/are exist 'there is' 'there was'

iw wn, nDs Ddi, rn.f there was, commoner Djedi, name.his 'behold there was a commoner, whose name was Djedi'

ist wn, Hmt.f Lo exists, wife.his 'He had a wife'

nty wn, wr, n wrw.f who/which exists, great-one, of great-ones.his 'who there existed a great one for his great ones'

The negation of 'existence' or 'non-existence' or absence' is by the use of **nn wn** 'there exists not' or 'there existed not':

nn wn, pHwy.fy not exist, end.it 'there is no end to it'

nn wn, mAr, n hAw.i not exist, wretch, of time.my 'there was none wretched in my time'

n wn, SsAw.sn(w) not exist, remedy.their 'there is no remedy for them'

nn mAatyw not, righteous 'there are no righteous'

nn, is-ib, dns sxr Xt not exist, light-heart, heavy counsel body 'There is none light hearted who is slow to move (heavy) regarding his bodily appetites' ie regarding the counsel of his body.

8.8 The negation nn may be translated as 'without, there is not':

di.sn(w), n.k, nHH, nn Drw.f, Dt nn Hnyt give.they, to.you, eternity, without end.its, eternity without period/end.it 'they give to you eternity without end and eternity without a period'

Haw rd, nn wn, mnt.f body vigorous, without, malady.its 'a healthy body, without sickness'

wAH xt, n wnt, Abw place-things (make offerings), without, cessation 'making offerings without ceasing'

VOCABULARY 8

Learn and write out from memory the following words in hieroglyphs, with transliteration and meaning:

mhy 'be neglectful, careless'

nDnD 'converse, take counsel'

HD 'be white, bright, white'

qd 'build'

Hm 'Majesty'

Hm 'Majesty'

sr 'official, noble'

HAty-a 'chieftan, local prince, mayor'

HAtyw-a 'Chieftans, princes, mayors'

bity 'king of Lower Egypt'

bAw 'might' plural

Snwt 'granary'

rnpt ‘year’

rk ‘time, period’

hAw ‘environment, neighbourhood, time’

sp ‘occasion, time, deed, fault’

bit ‘qualities, talent’

qd ‘form, character, good character, virtue’

Dr ‘end, limit’

mAr ‘wretched’

Dr ‘since’ (preposition)

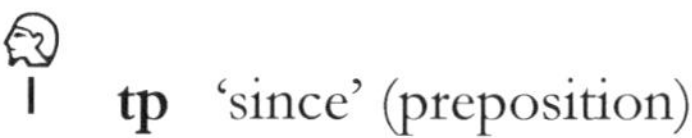

tp ‘since’ (preposition)

Study Note

Before proceeding remember to use your notebook to practice the alphabetic sound signs in lesson one. Repetition is key: by repeatedly hand drawing the signs in a stylised short-hand form with thier transliteration and sound you will gradually embed them in to your memory. Use up as many notebooks as you can when studying as repetition will also help you to develop your own hieroglyphic drawing technique.

EXERCISE 8

Transliterate and translate:

1.

2.

3.

4.

5.

6.

7.

8.

9.

LESSON 9

Demonstrative Adjectives and Pronouns

9.1 The Demonstratives

Words used and their historical variants to express 'this, that, the':

The masculine singular forms:

pw 'this' **pwy** 'this' **pn** 'this'

pf 'that' **pfy** 'that'

pfA 'that' **pA** 'this, the'

The feminine singular forms:

tw 'this' **twy** 'this'

tn 'this' **tf** 'that'

tfA 'that' **tA** 'the, this'

The plural common (neuter) forms:

nw 'this' **nn** 'this' **nn(n)** 'this'

nf 'that' **nfA** 'that' **nfA** 'that'

nA 'the, this'

Note: all the masculine forms begin with **p**, the feminine with **t** and the plural with **n**.
Earlier examples beginning with **i** of the plural forms which the student should be aware of:

ipw 'this' **ipn** 'this' **iptw** 'this' **iptn** 'this'

Generally the demonstratives 'this, that' follow their nouns, while **pA** and **tA** 'the' precedes it.

Study the following examples with word order exceptions:

ist tn place this 'this place'

hrw pfy day that 'that day'

pA Sfdw this/the papyrus-scroll 'this papyrus scroll'

pf gs that side 'that side'

tfA pXrt that remedy 'that remedy'

nn(n) srw these (of) officials 'these officials'

nA n awt these dwellings 'these dwellings'

nn n sxty this of peasant 'these peasants'

nn Hmwt these women 'these women'

Dd.n.f nn say.of.he this 'he said this'

pty nA what this 'what is this?'

ra pw Ra this/it-is 'this Ra (or) it is Ra'

pA pw Awsir the this Osiris 'This is the Osiris (or) such is Osiris'

rx.i pfA, r pn know.I that, from this 'I knew that from this'

Dd.in, sxty pn, n Hmt.f, tn said.by, peasant this, to wife.his, this 'Said by this peasant, to this his wife'

fnd.k, pw, Spss nose.your, this, noble 'this your noble nose'

nTr pwy aA god this great 'this great god'

HkAy pw magician this 'this magician'

xr pf enemy that 'that enemy!'

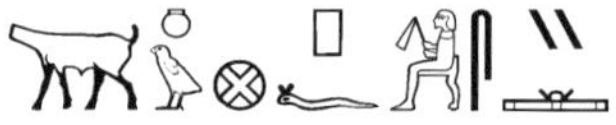

Xnw pf Spsy residence that noble 'that noble Residence'

tA spAt this district/nome 'this province'

nA n gmHwt this (plural) of candles 'these candles'

m tA At in this moment 'at this moment'

m pA hrw in this day 'on this day (or) today'

nA n it, nty-m, pA mXr this of corn, which-in, storehouse 'the corn which is in the store house'

9.2 Possessive Adjectives

The suffix pronouns are used for possession 'my, yours, theirs etc.' but also from the above demonstratives, **pA**, **tA** and **nA**, possive adjectives are derived.

These are used less frequently than the suffix pronouns, but the student should still be able to recognize and translate them correctly:

pAy.i 'my' with singular masculine noun

tAy.i 'my' with sing. fem. noun

nAy.i n 'my' with plur. noun

pAy.k 'your' with sing. masc. noun

tAy.k 'your' with sing. fem. noun

nAy.k n 'your' with plur. noun

Examples of use:

tAy.i Hmt this.my wife 'my wife'

nAy.s, n Xrdw this.her, of children 'her children'

9.3 The word iry 'thereto, thereof'

The word **iry** which is derived from **iry** 'relating to' is best translated as 'thereof, thereto':

Also used is: **irw** 'pertaining to' and the preposition: **xft** 'in front of, in accordance with, as well as, corresponding to'

Examples:

sA.f smsw, m Hry, iry son.his eldest, in-the-position-of chief, thereof 'his eldest son was the chief thereof'

hp irw law pertaining-to 'the law appertaining thereto'

xft iry according-to there-to 'according thereto'

Hr sA iry upon back thereof 'thereafter'

m-m iry therein relating-to 'among them'

m-xt iAw, n.k, imy after old-age, of.you, therein 'after your old age'

hdmw, n.sn, im(y) footstools, of.them, thereof 'footstools belonging to them'

9.4 Sentences Expressing Possession

Egyptian has no verb meaning 'to possess, to have or to belong to' this is expressed by use of the preposition **n** 'to' and its derivatives:

xt.i nbt, m SA niwt, n sn.i, iHy-snb property.my all, in country (and) town, **to** brother.my, Ihy-seneb 'all my property in country and town **(shall belong) to** my brother, Ihy-seneb'

wnn.s, n sbk-nxt exist.it, **to (for**) Sobek-nakhet 'It **(shall belong) to** Sobek-nakhet'

iw, n.k, anx is, **to**.you, life **to** you is, life 'you **shall have** life'

nn wn ib, n s not exist heart, to man 'no man has a heart'

nn is, n sbi, Hr Hm.f not tomb, **to/for** rebel, against Majesty.his 'there is no tomb for him-who-rebels against his Majesty'

nn n.k, st not to.you, it 'it does not belong to you'

Derivatives of the term for **n** 'belong to' are **ns sw** 'he belongs to' and **ns sy** 'it belongs to' using the biliteral sign **ns:**

ns 'belong to'

ns sw 'he/it belongs to' masc. **ns sy** 'she/it belongs to'

Examples of syntax showing possession:

ns s(y), imy-r pr it-belongs-to, overseer house 'it belongs to the overseer (steward) of the house'

ns sw, mH-30 belongs-to it, cubits-30 'it was 30 cubits (long)'

ntk nbw to-you gold 'to you belongs gold'

ink-sy she belongs to me 'Inuk-sy (a personal name)'

n.k, imy HD to.you, being-in silver (white gold) 'to you belongs silver'

antyw, n.i, im sw incense, to.i, therein it 'the incense, it belongs to me'

ist, wn Hmt.f lo, exist wife.his 'he has a wife'

nn wn, tp.f not exist, head.his 'he has no head'

n wnt, swwt.s not exist, reeds.it 'it has no reeds'

mk, tw m niwt, nn HqA.s behold, one in/as city, not ruler.it 'behold, not one in the city is a ruler'

VOCABULARY 9

Learn and write out from memory the following words in hieroglyphs, with transliteration and meaning:

biA 'marve'

by 'marvel'

xpr 'become, happen'

Xnm 'join, endure'

s-mn 'make firm, establish'

is 'tomb, tomb chamber'

sxnt 'supporting pole, support'

nbw 'gold'

HD 'silver'

HqA 'ruler, chieftain'

TAw 'breath, wind'

mrwt 'love'

Hryt 'apprehension, dread'

snD 'fear'

nDm 'be sweet, sweet, sweetness'

iwnn 'sanctuary'

iAmt 'charm, favour'

Snbt 'breast'

Ha 'piece of flesh, flesh (plural), body'

fnd 'nose'

sA 'magic knot, amulet, protection'

sA 'magic knot, amulet, protection'

At 'moment'

nDty 'helper, avenger'

EXERCISE 9

a) **Study** the following text:

The god Amen-Ra addresses the Pharaoh Tuthmosis III (Dynasty 18):

sA.i, nDty.i, (ra-mn-xpr) anx Dt
son.my, avenger.my (Ra-men-kheper) life eternal

'My son, my avenger, Menkheperra (may he) live eternally'

wbn.i, n mr(w)t.k
shine.I, of love.you

'I shine through love of you'

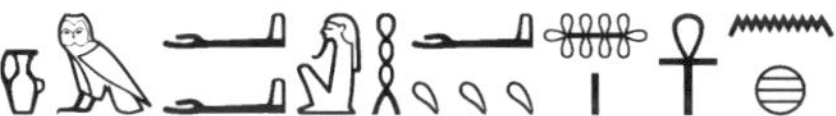

Xnm awy.i, Haw.k, m sA anx
endure/join hands.my, body.your, with protection life

'Join my hands and your body with the protection of life'

nDm.wy, iAmt.k, r Snbt.i
sweet-doubly, charm.your, to breast.i

'How sweet is your charm against my breast'

smn.i.tw, m iwnn.i
make-established.I.you, in sanctuary.my

'I established you in my sanctuary'

byA.i, n.k, di.i, bAw.k
marvel.I, at.you, place.I, might.your

'I marvel at you, I place your might...'

snDw.k, m tAw nbw
fear.your, in lands all

'(And) the fear of you in all lands'

Hryt.k, r Drw sxnwt, nt pt
dread.your, to limits (four) supports, of heaven

'The dread of you to the limits of the (four) supports of heaven'

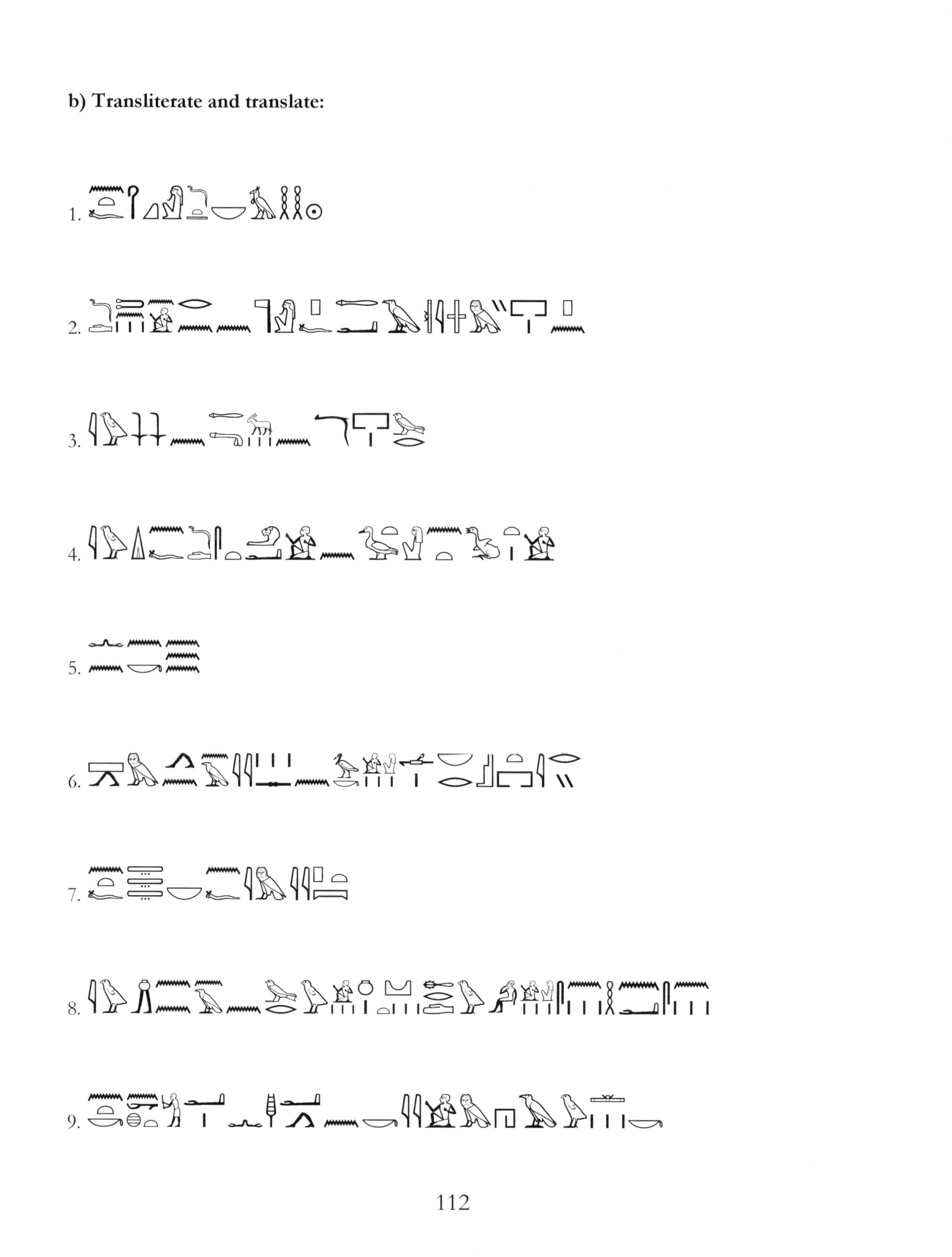

b) Transliterate and translate:

1.

2.

3.

4.

5.

6.

7.

8.

9.

LESSON 10

Further Study of Sentence Syntax

10.1 Sentence syntax examples for study:

ink Ds(.i), m Hawt I self(.my), in joy 'I myself was in joy'

HAty.i, n ntf, m Xt.i heart.my, not it, in body.my 'my heart, it was not in my body'

iw, Sdw.k, m sxt field-plots.your, in country 'behold (emphatic), your field plots are in the country'

iw, dAbw im.f, Hna iArrt behold, figs in.it, together-with grapes 'behold, figs were in it and also grapes'

10.2 The presence of iw at the start of a sentence:

The word **iw** 'behold, is, are' expresses emphasis at the beginning of a phrase or sentence, another word **ms** also expresses emphasis of a following statement:

ms expressing surprise or reproof

iw-ms 'untruth, mis-statement, but there is, forsooth!'

iw-ms, itrw m sfn forsooth!, river in/as blood 'forsooth, the river is blood!'

iw nA, m sbAyt is this, as instruction 'this is an instruction!'

10.3 Contrasting statements:

The following example expresses contrast between one statement and another:

'It was he who subdued foreign lands... **iw, it.f, m Xnw aH.f** behold, father.his, in interior castle.his '... (while), his father was within his castle'

iw, Xt.s, mi ntt sDt is, body.hers, like that under fire 'her body is like what is on fire'

When **iw** is omitted the statement becomes less emphatic:

Xrt.k, m pr.k rations.your, in house.your Translates simply as: 'your rations are in your house' a statement in the midst of an argumentative passage.

Part of a description:

dqrw nb, Hr xtw.f fruit all/any, upon trees.its 'all kinds of fruit were upon its trees'

psSw m awnw divider (of property) as (in-the-position-of) plunderer 'the apportioner (of property) is now a spoiler'

'Every man was caused to know his order of march...' **Htr, m-sA, Htr** horse, following-after, horse '...horse after horse'

ib.i, m sn-nw.i heart.my, as second.my '...my heart being my (only) companion (my second)'

iw.i, Xr Hswt, nt nsw xr is.I, under favours, of king under 'I was in receipt of favours from the king'

iw.f, m imy-Hat, n irr is.he, as pattern/mode-of-conduct, of doer (criminal) 'he is a pattern for the criminal'

'A storm went forth...' **iw.n, m wAD-wr** are.we, in Green-Great '...(while) we were in the Great-green (the great sea, the Mediterranean)'

iw.f, m nsw is.he, as king '(Now that) he is king'

10.4 Sentences expressing tense and mood:

Dd.Tn(w), Taw n anx, r fnD, n wAHy sbk-Htp say.you, breath of life, to nose, of Wahy Sobek-Hetep 'you shall say: the breath of life (be) to the nose of Wahy Sobekhotep'

nn rn.f, m-m anxw not name.his, among living 'his name shall not be among the living'

The **future tense** is often expressed by the use of the **wnn.f** 'exist.of.he' form 'exist.it, exist.my' etc:

wnn.f, tAy.i, Hmt im exist.it, my (possessive 'my' ie 'this-my'), wife therein 'my wife shall be there'

wnn.f, m xbd, n ra exist-of.he, in disfavour, of Ra 'he shal be in the disfavour of Ra'

The **wn.f** 'exist.he' form is also used in order to express *purpose*:

ii.n.(i), wn.(i), m sA.T come.of.(I), exist.(I), as protection.your 'I have come that I may be your protection'

The **wn.f** form is also used after the words **ix** 'then, therefore' and **rdi** 'cause' to express *purpose*:

ix wn.i, m Sms, n nTr therefore be.I, in following, of god 'therefore let me be in the following of the god'

rdi.n.s, wn.k, m nTr cause.of.she, be.you, as god 'she caused you to be a god'

10.5 SYNTAX OF PARTICLES

Particles are words which do not fit into the usual grammatical definitions, they usually start a sentence and add meaning or emphasis, such as 'behold', 'lo', 'when', 'now' etc.

Syntax in Egyptian with the word mk 'behold':

mk.k 'behold you' sing. masc. or general

mk.T 'behold you' sing. fem.

mk.Tn 'behold you' plural

mk.tn(w) 'behold you' plural

Example syntax:

mtn Spswt, Hr Sdw behold noble-ladies, upon rafts 'behold, noble ladies are (now) on rafts' ie deprived of their luxury boats

mk wi, r-gs.k behold I, at-side-your 'behold I am in your company'

mk tw, m minw behold you, as herdsman 'behold you are a herdsman'

Syntax in Egyptian with the words isT or ist or sT

These are forms which are related to the enclitical particle **is** 'lo', 'indeed' and express a situation of fact:

'I spent many years under king Antef... **isT, tA pn, Xr st-Hr.f** lo, land this, under charge.his '(while) this land was under his charge, ...'

sT.w(i), m bAk.f lo.I, as servant.his '... while I was (as) his servant'

'In year 30... **ist Hm.f, Hr xAst rTnw** lo majesty.his, upon country Retjnu '... lo his majesty was in the land of Retjnu'

The enlcitic particle rf

A reminder that the enclitic particle **rf** 'then, now' is used for emphasis in statements, also with wishes, commands and questions, following after **isT** the meaning may be translated as 'now!'

The use of **isT-rf** to express the meaning 'now':

isT-rf lo-emphasis 'now, when'

Example:

ist-rf, pr DHwty-nxt pn, Hr smA-tA now, house Djhwty-nakhet this, upon river-bank 'Now this house of Djhwty-nakhet was on the river-bank'

The words isk and sk:

These are archaic variations of **isT** and **st** and have the same meaning:

isk 'now, when' **sk** 'now, when'

Examples syntax:

isk Hm.s, m inpw when majesty.her, as royal-child 'when her majesty was a royal child'

sk wi, m Smsw.f when I, as following-after.his 'when I was in his following'

In Egyptian the word ti has a similar meaning to isT:

ti 'now, then'

Example syntax:

ti sw, Hr pri when he, upon battle-field 'when he was upon the battle-field'

'I knew your qualities... **ti wi, m sSy** when I, in nest '...when I was in the nest'

ti Hm.f, Ds.f, Hr xtm iAbty lo/when majesty.his, self.him, in fortress eastern 'lo, His Majesty was in the eastern fortress.'

The words xr or ixr:

These indicate what comes next in order and may be translated as 'and', 'further', or even sometimes as 'accordingly', 'so':

xr 'and, further, accordingly, so' **ixr** 'and, further, accordingly, so'

ixr 'and, further, accordingly, so'

Example:

xr, r-5 r-15, m wAh, Hr f so, 1/5 + 1/15, in place, upon.it 'so, 1/5+1/15 is what-is-to-be-added to it'

The rare word **nHmn** which means 'assuredly' may also be used as a particle to qualify a following statement:

mHmn wi, mi kA assuredly I, like bull 'assuredly I am like a bull'

The particle **HA** expresses a wish 'wish, would that':

HA n.i, Ssp nb, mnx would-that to.me, image/statue any, efficient/beneficent/excellent 'would that (wish) I had (to me) any beneficent idol.'

The sign group **Hwy-A** also expresses a wish:

Hwy-A wi im wish I there 'Would that I were there or I wish I were there'

10.6 Negation of Sentences

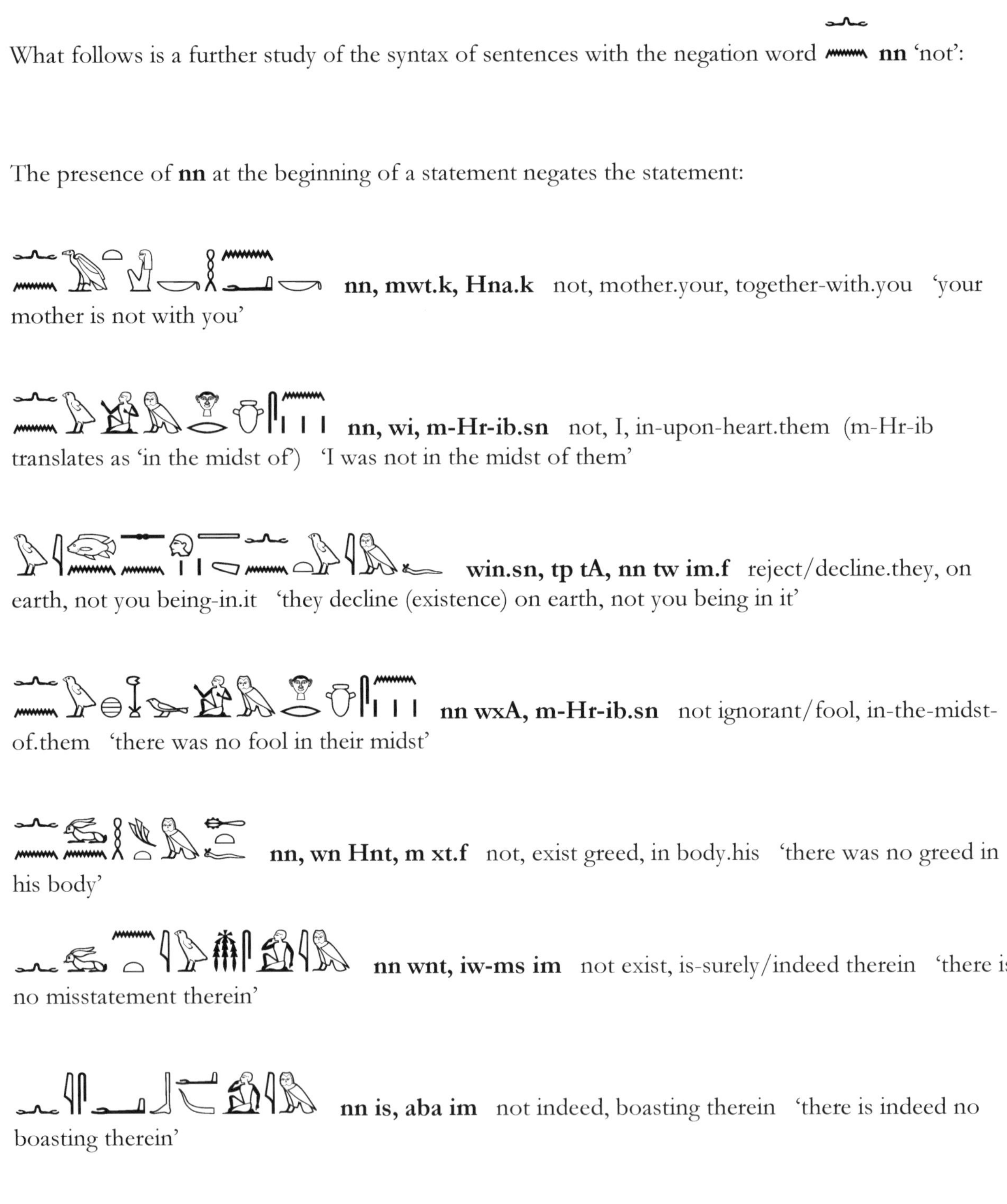

What follows is a further study of the syntax of sentences with the negation word **nn** 'not':

The presence of **nn** at the beginning of a statement negates the statement:

nn, mwt.k, Hna.k not, mother.your, together-with.you 'your mother is not with you'

nn, wi, m-Hr-ib.sn not, I, in-upon-heart.them (m-Hr-ib translates as 'in the midst of') 'I was not in the midst of them'

win.sn, tp tA, nn tw im.f reject/decline.they, on earth, not you being-in.it 'they decline (existence) on earth, not you being in it'

nn wxA, m-Hr-ib.sn not ignorant/fool, in-the-midst-of.them 'there was no fool in their midst'

nn, wn Hnt, m xt.f not, exist greed, in body.his 'there was no greed in his body'

nn wnt, iw-ms im not exist, is-surely/indeed therein 'there is no misstatement therein'

nn is, aba im not indeed, boasting therein 'there is indeed no boasting therein'

nn iw.k, m pt not is/are.you, in heaven 'you are not in heaven'

n wnn, sA.f, Hr nst.f not exist/be, son.his, upon seat.his 'his son shall not be upon his seat'

Study the word syntax of the following examples:

rmw im, Hna Apdw fish therein, together-with birds 'fish were there together with birds'

HAty.k, n.k, n imy-Hat heart.your, to.you, of being-in-front 'Your heart is to you of being in front'

10.7 Use of the preposition r to indicate a future condition:

iw.f, r smr is.he, to (towards) companion he is towards a companion 'he shall be a companion'

mT sw, r wnmw behold it, to food 'behold, it is for food'

In the following examples of syntax the subject of the sentence is missing but inferred:

iw, mi sxt nTr behold, (it) like counsel (of) god '(It) was like the counsel of the god'

nn, m iw-ms, xft-Hr.Tn not, as untruth, in-front-of.you '(This) is not as falsehood before you'

nn wn, Hr-xw.f not exist, upon-exclusion.him 'there was none beside him'

n Dd, HA n.i, r xt nb not say, would-that to.i, concerning thing any 'I did not say, 'would that to me about anything" or 'I did not say, 'Would that I had, about anything'

10.8 Use of the personal pronoun tw.i and its derivatives:

tw.i 'I' 1st person common

tw.k 'You' 2nd person masculine

tw.t 'you' 2nd person feminine

sw 'he, it' 3rd person masculine

sy 'she, it' 3rd person feminine

tw.tw 'one' impersonal

tw.n(w) 'we' 1st person plural

tw.tn(w) 'you' 2nd pers. com. plur.

st(w) 'they' 3rd pers. com. plur.

Example syntax:

sw Xr tA, n aAmw, tw.n(w) Xr kmt he under land, of Asiatics, we under Egypt 'he is in possession (under) land of the Asiatics, we are in possession (under) of Egypt'

sy m Hr.f, mi tA pt it in face.his, like the sky it in his face, like the sky 'it seemed to him like heaven'

VOCABULARY 10

Learn and write out from memory the following words in hieroglyphs, with transliteration and meaning:

bT 'abandon, forsake'

sb 'send, pass (time)'

km 'complete, completion'

skA 'plough, cultivate'

Hmw 'rudder'

Apd 'bird'

Apd 'bird'

rm 'fish'

AHt 'field'

Abd 'month'

iAt 'office, rank'

iAt 'office, rank'

, , **nst** 'seat'

, **Hb** 'festival, holiday'

Sms ‘follow, accompany, serve’

, **Smsw** ‘following, suite (noun)’

iAw ‘old’

iAwt ‘old age’

hnw ‘jubilation, praise’

r-pr ‘temple, chapel, shrine’

Hwt ‘house, large edifice’

nTr-Hwt ‘god-house ie temple’ spoken **Hwt-nTr**

HAty ‘heart, breast’

iw ‘wrong, crime’

qA ‘high, tall’

qAq ‘height’

EXERCISE 10

Transliterate and translate:

1.

2.

3.

4.

5.

6.

7.

8.

9.

10.

STUDY 10.1

The Offering Formula of the Funerary Cult

Food offerings in tombs and temples were called:

irt Htp-di-nsw

make/do king offering give

'Making an offering which the king gives'

ie performing the **Htp-di-nsw** 'an offering which the king gives'

In the case of a dead king, the one making the offering is in theory Horus, the son and heir of the dead Osiris king and stands with arms raised in the attitude of invocation, 'calling, invoking' before the shrine, statue or stela of the god or deceased parent:

nis 'calling, invoking'

An example of the **Htp-di-nsw** formula:

nsw-Htp-di Awsir, nb Ddw, nTr aA, nb AbDw

king-offering-gives Osiris, lord Djedu, god great, lord Abedju

di.f, prt-xrw: t Hnqt, kAw Apdw, Ss mnxt

gives.he, invocation-offerings: bread beer, oxen fowl, alabaster clothing

xt nbt, nfr wab, anxt nTr im

things all, good pure, lives god therein

n kA n, imAxy, wsrt-sn, mAa-xrw

to ka of, venerated, Wasret-Sen, True-Voice

'An offering which the king gives (to) Osiris, Lord of Busiris, the great god, lord of Abydos, that he may give invocation offerings of bread and beer, oxen and fowl, alabaster and clothing, all things good and pure on which a god lives, to the ka (spirit) of the revered Sen-wasret, justified.'

The food offerings made by the living pharaoh in the pyramid-temple of his deceased father or predecessor were likewise known as the **nsw-Htp** 'an offering of the king'. Other gods, such as Anubis, the god of embalming and Geb, the earth-god, were also givers of similar offerings.

In the Old Kingdom we find on almost every funerary false door or lintel formulae such as the following:

nsw-Htp-di, inpw-Htp (di), xnty nTr-sH, tpy Dw.f

king-offering-gives, Inpw-offering-(gives), in-front divine-booth, upon mountain.his

prt-xrw n.f, m H b ra, nb, ptH-Spss

invocation-offerings for.him, in festival day, every, ptH-Spss

'An offering which the king gives, and an offering (of) Anubis, in front of the divine booth, he who is upon his mountain, that there may be invocation offerings for him at every festival and every day, Ptah-shepses.'

In the Old Kingdom the phrase **Htp-di-nsw** is followed by **Htp-di-Inpw** (or **Awsir** or **gb**) 'a offering which Anubis (Or Osiris or Geb) gives.' Frequently **Htp-di-Inpw** is substituted with:

inpw Htp Anubis offering 'Offering which Anubis gives'

Variations of the offering formula following after the phrase **Htp-di-nsw** and name of one god were used from the Middle Kingdom onwards: **di.f** if one god is named and **di.sn(w)** if several gods are named:

di.f 'that he may give' **di.sn(w)** 'that they may give'

The main idea behind the offering formula is that: the king gives, or has given, or is to give, an offering to some god in his temple, in order that the latter in turn may give offerings to a private individual in his tomb.

Of the vast amounts of food offerings accumulating in the temples only a small proportion was consumed by the priests, the rest was distributed to the persons in charge of private funerary cults who were known as **Hmw-kA** 'servants of the ka, soul-priests':

Hmw-kA 'servants of the ka, soul priests'

In Middle Egyptian: **nsw-Htp-di** 'an offering which the king gives'

The expression **prt-xrw** 'invocation offerings' seems to come from the phrase: **pr xrw** 'the voice goes forth':

pr xrw go-forth voice 'the voice goes forth'

Variations, abbreviations and examples of the offering formula:

di.f, prt-xrw, m t, m Hnqt

gives.he, invocation-offerings, as bread, as beer

'That he may give invocation offerings consisting of bread and of beer'

Abbreviations and full spellings used in invocation offering formula:

, **kAw** 'oxen'

, **Apdw** 'fowl'

, **Ss** 'alabaster'

, **mnxt** 'clothing'

The Deceased's Ka

In Middle Egyptian the funerary offerings are made **n kA n** 'to the ka of' the deceased. In this context the word kA is translated as 'spirit, soul, personality,' of the person.

n kA n 'to the ka of'

STUDY 10.2

Number and Measurement

In ancient Egyptian the writing of numbers is similar in style to that later used by the Romans using a series of strokes and signs.

The Writing of Numerals

A single vertical stroke is used for the units which are combined with special signs for various powers of ten:

I **wa** '1, one' **wa** '1, one' ∩ **mD(w)** '10, ten'

Stt '100, one hundred' **xA** '1000, thousand' **Dba** '10,000, ten thousand'

Hfn '100,000, hundred thousand' **HH** '1,000,000, million'

Numbers are made up by additions of the above signs, the higher value signs are written in front of the lower. Repetition of the signs is used to indicate any value of number:

II **2** III **3** IIIIII **6** ∩∩IIII **24** ∩∩∩∩∩∩II **62** **2,023**

Hence the number 152,123 is represented by:

The number 966 by:

The names of numbers:

1	wa	2	snwy
3	xmtw	4	fdw
5	diw	6	sisw or srsw
7	sfxw	8	xmnw
9	psDw	10	mDw
20	Dbaty	30	mabA
40	Hm	50	diyw
60	srsyw or sisyw	70	sfxyw
80	xmnyw	90	psDyw
100	St	1,000	xA
10,000	Dba	100,000	Hfn

Cardinal Numbers

Examples of the use of cardinal numbers: the general rule is that the number follows the noun:

mH 1 cubit-1 'one cubit'

sDm.f 2 ears.his 2 'his two years'

s 3 man 3 'three men'

rnpt 20 years 20 'twenty years'

HfAw 75 snakes 75 'seventy five snakes'

Hnwt ds 100 beer jugs 100 'one hundred jugs of beer'

dmi 1000 towns 1000 'thousand towns'

s(w) 10,000 man 10,000 'ten thousand men'

spw 4 times/occasions 4 'four times'

st-Hmt women 20 'twenty women'

iHw 618 cattle 618 'six hundred and eighteen (head of) cattle'

pA s(w) 2 the man 2 'the two men'

hrw 3 pn day 3 this 'these three days'

tA it HqAt 6 the corn heqat 6 'the six heqats of corn'

pA.i Xrdw 4 this.my children 4 'this my four children'

3 pn 3 this 'these three'

pA 21 the 21 'the twenty one'

tA t(w) 100 the loves 100 'the hundred loaves'

tA t(w) 1000 the loaves 1000 'the thousand loaves'

ky nHsy 6 another Nubian 6 'another six Nubians'

kt 100, sA kt 100 another 100, behind another 100 'one hundred, after another one hundred'

The word wa 'one':

dmi wa city one 'one city'

wAt.f wat side.its one 'its one side'

wa n mTn one of road 'one road'

waw n qAqAw one of ship 'a ship'

wa im.Tn nb one in.your every 'every one of you'

The words for 1,000 and 1,000,000 are sometimes written before the noun:

xA m t Hnqt thousand as bread beer 'a thousand of bread and beer'

xA.k pn, n rnpt thousand.your, of years 'this your thousand of years'

m HH pn, rnpwt in million this, years 'in this million of years'

120 nt xA-tAw 120 of thousand-land 'one hundred and twenty thousands-of-land' a land measure

tA 365 n nTr the 365 of gods 'the 365 gods'

35 n rnpt 35 of years '35 years'

Ordinal Numbers

1. The Ordinal for First

For the word , **tpy** ‘first’ the sign **tp** ‘head’ is used and usually follows the noun:

Variations: , , **tpy** ‘first’

sp tpy time first ‘the first time’

wDyt tpt campaign first ‘the first campaign’

2. The Ordinals for 2 to 9

These are formed by the addition of an ending: **nw** (masculine) and **nwt** (feminine) and the prefix **mH** for numbers 10 and over:

For example:

II	**snw**	‘two’	II	**snw-nw**	‘second’
III	**xmt**	‘three’	III	**xmt-nw**	‘third’
III III	**sisw**	‘six’	III III	**sisw-nw**	‘sixth’

Examples of use of the ordinals:

fdw-nw sp fourth time 'the fourth time'

m sn-nwt.f, iAt in second.his, office 'in his second office'

Hr sn-nw.sy for second.it 'for its second (time)' ie 'again'

sp.f, 3-nw Hb-sd time.his, third Jubilee 'his third time of Jubilee'

wDyt 6-nwt expedition sixth 'the sixth expedition'

5-nw n Hb fifth of festival 'the fifth festival'

For numbers 10 and upwards the ordinals are formed with the words **mH** (masculine) and **mHt** (feminine) meaning 'filling, completing:

wDyt mHt-10 campaign tenth the tenth campaign'

Sometimes the cardinals can appear as ordinals as in dates of events, for example, 'year 2' may be written as the 'second year':

HAt-sp 2, Abd 2, Axt hrw 16 year 2, month 2, inundation-season day 16 'Regnal year 2, day 16 of the second month of the season of inundation'

tpy n Axt first of inundation 'first (month) of inundation-season'

Abd 4 n Smw month 4 of summer 'the fourth month of summer'

arqy 'last (thirtieth) day of the month'

aHa.n.i, xd.kwi, Hr Sms, m 6 n Xnw

arise.of.i, fare-downsteam.you, with follow, as 6 of residence

'I sailed downstream in the following as six of the residence'

Number Fractions

The method of expressing fractions was by the use of the word **r** 'part' below which was the number denominator:

r-3 part-3 '1/3 ie one third'

r-273 part-273 '1/273'

The Corn Measure

The parts of the sound eye of Horus represented fraction:

wDAt 'sound left eye of Horus'

	1/2	'a half a heqat'
	1/4	'a quarter a heqat'
	1/8	'one eighth a heqat'
	1/16	'one sixteenth of a heqat'
	1/32	'one thirty second of a heqat'
	1/64	'one sixty fourth of a heqat'

The **heqat** being a measure of corn = 4.54 litres.

These fractions together add up to 63/64 and are employed with the heqat (**HqAt**) measure:

, , , , or **HqAt** heqat 'measure, 4.5 litres'

Measure of Length

Measurement of length is given in cubits, where 1 cubit = 20.6 inches = 0.523 metres.

One cubit = 7 palms = 28 digits. 100 cubits = 1 rod.

mH	‘cubit’	**xt**	‘rod, of 100 cubits’

Ssp ‘palm = 1/7 cubit’

DbA ‘finger, finger breadth = 1/28 cubit’

xt-n-nwH ‘rod-of-cord, 100 cubits in length’

sXb.xr.f, mH 1, Ssp 3, m mw aAw

swallow.by.it, cubit 1, palm 3, in water great

‘It swallows 1 cubit and 3 palms of the great waters’

mH 4, Abd 4, Dba 2

'four cubits, four palms and two digits'

swsx.n.i, wAt n wDHw.i, m xt-n-nwH 21

widen.of.i, road of offerings.my, as rod-of-cord 21

'I made wide the road for my offerings as twenty one rods of cord (2,100 cubits)'

AHt n xt 10, r xt 2

field of rods 10, by rods 2

'A field of 10 rods by 2 rods'

A much larger measure of length is the **itrw** 'river-measure' (Greek: schoenus) and is estimated to be 20,000 cubits = 10.5 km:

itrw 'river-measure'

Measures of Area

, sTAt 'Greek: aroura, a field measure of about 2/3 acre, 100 cubits squared'

sTA 'measure of capacity'

The **sTAt measure** equals: 1 **xt** by 1 **xt** = 1 rod by 1 rod = 100 cubits by 100 cubits. 1 **sTAt** = 2735 square metres approx 2/3 acre.

The fractions of the **sTAt** are the **rmn** which equals ½ **sTAt**

The × **Hsb** = ¼ **sTAt**, and the **sA** = 1/8 **sTAt**

Smaller parts of the aroura are expressed in terms of the length of the cubit, the **mH** 'cubit' is a strip of land 100 cubits by 1 cubit = 1/100 **sTAt**.

A larger measure of 10 arouras (1000 by 1000 cubits) is written as **xA-tA**:

xA-tA '10 arouras = 1000 by 1000 cubits'

Aht, xA 2, sTat 2 field, 10-arouras 2, aroura 2 'twenty two arouras of field'

|||| || **4 sTAt, 2 rmn** 'forty two and a half arouras'

[sTAt 8 + rmn (1/2 sTAt) + Hsb (1/4 sTAt) + zA (1/8 sTAt)] + [mH (1/100 cubit) 10 + gs (1/2) + Hsb (1/4)]

[8 + ½ + ¼ + 1/8 = 8 7/8 arouras] + [1/10 + ½ + ¼ = 10 ¾ cubits]

'8 7/8 arouras, 10 ¾ cubits'

Measures of Weight

The weight employed for metals was the **dbn** 'deben' and had a weight of about 91 grams, the **qdt**, **kite** was 1/10 of a deben.

dbn 'deben, measure of weight = 91 grams'

qdt 'kite, 1/10 deben'

Saty 'Seal, measure of value or weight (of gold or silver), 1/12 of a deben weighing 7.6 grams'

iH 1, irw n Saty 8 ox 1, make of seals 8 'One ox, making eight seals'

STUDY 10.3

The divisions of Time and Method of Dating

The Egyptian year (**rnpt**) was divided into 12 months (**Abd**) of 30 days (**hrw**) making 360 days, the addition of 5 extra days, the epagomenal 'added' days, made up the year of 365 days.

rnpt 'year' **Abd** 'month'  **hrw** 'day'

Hryw-rnpt 'added 5 (epagomenal) days'

The year was further divided into three seasons of four months each:

tr 'season, of 4 months'  **Axt** 'inundation season'

prt 'winter, season of emergence, of the fields from the flood water'

Smw 'summer, season of deficiency of water'

HAt-sp 'regnal year, of the king' **sw** 'day'

Example syntax:

HAt-sp 2, Abd 3, Axt, sw 1, xr Hm, n nsw-bit (n-mAat-ra)

regnal-year 2, month 3, inundation-season, day 1, under majesty, of K.U.L.E (En-maat-Ra)

'Regnal year 2, third month of inundation, day one under the Majesty of King of Upper and Lower Egypt (En-maat-ra)'

m Hat-sp 24, Abd 2, prt, arqy, hrw-Hb mH-10, n Imn, m Ipt-swt

in regnal-year 24, month 2, winter-season, last-day, day-festival-10, of Amun, in Ipet-sut

'In year 24, second month of winter, last day, tenth festival day of Amun in Ipet-sut (Karnak)'

tpy Axt, wpt-rnpt, Hb Xnmw

first month (of) inundation, opening-of-the year, festival Xenum

'First month of inundation, opening of the year (= day 1), feast of Khenum'

During the early dynasties of ancient Egypt dates were not assigned to the regnal years of the king, but instead dates were tied to some specific event.

During the 5th and 6th dynasties a biennial event, the cattle census, was used:

Hat-sp 14, Tnwt iH, awt nb

beginning-year 14, number (of) oxen, small-cattle (sheep, goats) all

'Beginning of time 14, of the numbering of the oxen and all of the small cattle like sheep and goats'

rnp m-xt sp 18

year, accompanying/after time 18

'The beginning after time 18'

Hours of the Day and Night

The Egyptians were the first to divide the day into 24 hours, there were twelve hours of day and twelve hours of the night.

 **wnwt** 'hour'

 **wnwty** 'hour-watcher, star-watcher'

wnwt mHt-10, nt hrw

hour ten, of day

'The tenth hour of the day'

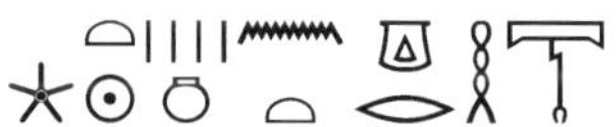

wnwt 4-nwt, nt grt

hour 4, of night

'The fourth hour of the night'

SECTION II

Reading Ancient Egyptian Art

Study 2.1

Cartouches of the Kings

Reading the hieroglyphic text which accompanies the artistic images in tombs and on temples, stela and other various monuments brings the ancient Egyptians to life. The first thing we usually translate is the name of the owner of the tomb, temple or monument. The names of royalty are usually enclosed in a cartouche. The ancient Egyptian word for cartouche was **shenew** and was an elongated form of the **shen-ring**. The word **shen** itself means, in ancient Egyptian 'encircle', while the shen-ring represented eternal protection. In its elongated form the shen-ring became the cartouche which enclosed and protected a royal name:

Sn *determinative in words: 'surround, encircle'

Snw **'**surround, encircle, circuit, cartouche'

Snw 'cartouche'

Snw 'cartouche'

The cartouche came into use under the fourth dynasty pharaoh Sneferu:

snfrw 'Senefru'

The following is a cartouche king list of some pharaohs of the dynastic period from Sneferu onwards.

4th Dynasty Old Kingdom

xwfw **'**Khufu (Greek: Cheops)'

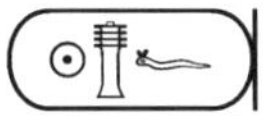

Dd-f-ra 'Djedefra'

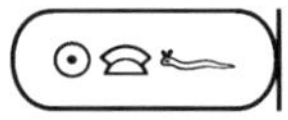

xa-f-ra 'Khafra'

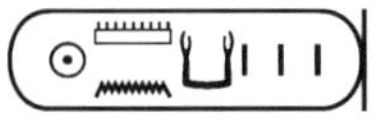

mn-kA-w-ra 'Menkarura'

Spss-kA-f 'Shepseskhaf'

Note: although the sun disc, the sun god Ra, is written first in honour that he is a god of the king, his name comes last in the pharaoh's name.

5th Dynasty Old Kingdom

wAs-ka-f 'Userkaf' **sA-w-ra** 'Sahura'

n-wAs-ra 'Enuserra'

Inscription on a red sandstone block bearing the name of Enuserra at his Sun Temple - Abu Gurab:

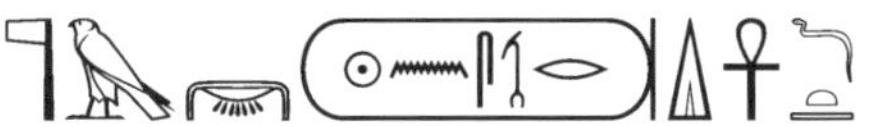

nTr Hr nbw (n-wAsr-ra) di anx Dt

god Horus gold (Enuserra) given life forever

'The god Horus of Gold, Nuserra, may he be given Life forever'

11th Dynasty Middle Kingdom

 **mnTw-Htp** 'Mentjuhotep'

12th Dynasty Middle Kingdom

 **sA ra, imn-m-HAt** 'Son of Ra, Amenemhet'

 **sA ra, sn-wsrt** 'Son of Ra, Senuseret'

18th Dynasty New Kingdom

 **sA ra, iaH-ms** 'Son of Ra, Amose'

 **sA ra, DHwty-ms** 'Son of Ra, Djhutymose (Thutmose)'

 **sA ra, Hat-Sps-w** 'Son of Ra, Hatshepsut'

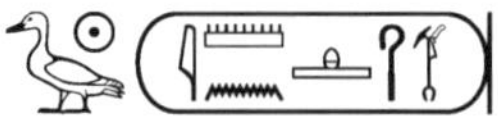 **sA ra, imn-Htp, HqA wAs** 'Son of Ra, Amunhotep, Ruler of Thebes'

 **sA ra, twt-anx-imn, HqA iwn Sma** 'Son of Ra, Tut-ankh-amun, Ruler of Thebes'

Study 2.2

The Tomb of Tutankhamun

New Kingdom 18th Dynasty 1332-1323 BC.

Tuankhamun's Names and Titles

1. His Son of Ra (birth name):

The name given to the king before accession to the throne, which is equivalent to a family name:

sA ra (twt-anx-imn HqA iwn Sma)

son Ra (Tut-ankh-Amun, Prince (of) Pillar-Town Southern

'Son of Ra, Tutankhamun, Ruler of Thebes'

The name **Tut-ankh-amun** translates as 'Image-living (of) Amun' ie 'Living image of Amun.' In fact, this was not his original birth name, at Amarna and under the reign of his grandfather (or father) Amenhotep III, he is known as Tut-ankh-aten, 'The Living Image of the Aten' which is interesting since after Amenhotep III deified himself as a god he was known as the Glorious Aten.

The gold throne chair of Tutankhamun has his cartouche names inlaid with semi-precious stones and on the left arm of the chair is his throne name: **Neb-kheper-u-ra**, but on the right arm is his birth name, **Tutankhaten**:

twt-anx-itn (sun-disk* for x)

Tut-ankh-aten

* Note: the scribe has used a sun-disk in place of the usual **x** sign, the cartouche would normally be written as:

In this case the scribe may be emphasising the aspects of the solar worship of the (sun-disk) god, the Aten, thus reinforcing the Tutankhaten's name with the religion of Amarna.

2. The Prenomen Throne (Nsw-bity) Name

nsw-bit (xpr-w-nb-ta)

KNS (Kheper-u-neb-Ra)

'The King of Upper and Lower Egypt (Neb-kheper-u-ra)'

The name **Neb-Kheper-u-ra** translates as 'Ra, Lord of created-forms.'

3. Horus Name

This name was often written inside a rectangular frame, a serekh, which was a representation of the palace courtyard and facade. The falcon god Horus perches on top of the serekh and the king's Horus name represented the king as the earthly incarnation of the ancient falcon god, Horus.

Hr [kA-nxt-twt-mswt]

Horus [bull strong, image births]

'Horus (king) [Kanakhet-tut-mesut]'

4. Nebty (Two-Ladies) Name

nbty, nfr-hpw, s-grH tAwy

Two-Ladies, good laws, quelled two-lands

'Nebty: Nefer-hepu-segereh-tawy'

5. The Golden Horus Name

The Golden Horus name of the king may represent the victory of Horus over his enemy Seth.

Hr-nbw, wTs-xaw, s-Htp-nTrw

Horus-Gold, wear/carry-shining-crown, made-satisfied-gods

Golden Horus: Wearer of the Shining Crown, who made satisfied the gods

'The Golden Horus: Wetjes-khau-sehetep-netjeru'

North wall of the burial chamber

The large painting on the north wall shows Tutankhamun in three separate scenes. On the far right the Sem priest wearing the blue war crown and dressed in the traditional leopard skin performs the opening of the mouth ceremony on the deceased Osiris King Tutankhamun.

This ceremony was usually performed by the deceased's son and heir, in this case the following king, Ay performs the right which secures his position as the next pharaoh.

The middle scene shows Tutankhamun as the living king being greeted by the goddess Nut into the realm of the gods. In the left scene wearing the nemes headdress Tutankhamun is followed behind by his ka, his spiritual double, and is welcomed by Osiris, king of the dead.

Right scene enlarged – North Wall

Left register over Tutankhamun

nTr nfr, nb tAwy, nb xaw nsw bit (xpr-w-nb-ra)

god good, lord two-lands, lord appearances KNS (Neb-kheper-u-ra)

'The good god, lord of the two-lands and lord of appearances,

King of Upper and Lower Egypt, Neb-kheper-u-ra'

Right register over Ay

nTr nfr, nb tAwy, nb irt xt, nsw-bit (xprw*-ra)

god good, lord two-lands, lord doing things, KNS (Kheperura)

'The good god, lord of the Two-Lands, lord of doing things (Kheper-u-ra)

* Note: in Ay's cartouche the plural (**w**) of **xpr-w** is expressed by the repetition of three signs, in other places his name reads: 'Kheper-kheper-u-ra.'

Middle scene north wall

Right register over Tutankhamun

nb tAwy (nb-xpr-w-ra) di anx DtA HH

lord two-lands (Neb-kheper-u-ra) given life eternal forever

'Lord of the Two-Lands, Neb-kheper-u-ra, may he be given life eternal forever'

Left register over the goddess Nut

nwt, nbt pt, (H)nwt nTrw, ir.s, nyny, ms n.s

Nut, lady heaven, mistress gods, make.she, greeting! born of.her

di.s, snb anx, r--.k, anx ti DtA

give.she, health life, --.you, life you forever

'Nut, Lady of Heaven, mistress of the gods, she makes greeting to (him) born of her, may she be given health and life ... you, life for you forever'

Left scene – north wall

Right register – above Tutankhamun's Ka – identifying his ka name

Hr wADt, ka-nxt, ka

Horus Cobra-goddess, Bull-strong/victorious, Soul-Double

'Horus and Wadjet, Victorious Bull, Soul-double'

nsw tA-wr n, xntt bHdt

king nome-of-Abydos, foremost (of) Edfu-temple

'King of Abydos, foremost of Edfu Temple'

The South Wall

The south wall depicts the deceased Tutankhamun, who is wearing the **khat** headdress, being welcomed into the realm of the gods. On his right and facing him is the goddess Hathor who is holding the sign of life, the ankh, to his nose, the seat (breath) of life.

To his immediate left is the jackal headed god, Anubis, the god of embalming. Anubis greets Tutankhamun by placing his left hand upon his shoulder.

The south wall (left) – West wall (right)

To the left of Anubis stands the goddess Isis ready to greet Tutankhamun to the underworld with the gift of water, the water is represented by the the **mu** sign which she holds in each hand. Behind her, sit three minor deities.

Register above Hathor

Hwt-Hr, nbt pt, Hry-tp DAtt imnt

Hat-hor, lady heaven, chieftain estate west

'Hathor, lady of heaven, chief of the estate of the west'

The estate of the west side of the Nile, where the sun sets for its journey to the underworld is the burial necropolis of tombs and temples.

Register above Tutankhamun's head

nTr nfr (nb-xpr-w-ra) di anx DtA HH

god good (Neb-kheper-u-ra) given life eternal forever

'The good god, Neb-kheper-u-ra, may he be given eternal life forever'

Right of Anubis's Head

inpw, xntt imnt, nTr nfr, im..t, nb pt

Inpu, foremost west, god good, who-is-in?, lord heaven

'Anubis, foremost of the west, lord of heaven'

Part of the West Wall

This scene depicts twelve baboon deities of the twelve hours of the night (6 shown) through which the solar bark and the king must travel through before reaching rebirth at dawn.

The top register shows the sung god Khepri in a solar bark, either side are two worshiping deities.

dwA xpr dwA

'adore Khepri adore'

Awsir xpr Awsir

'Osiris Khepri Osiris'

The names of the baboon deities: read right to left and down: Note: the lighter text written in red is read first followed by the darker text written in black:

Hkn m bs'f, nis m bs.f
acclaim as flame.his, call as flame.his

'Extol as Besef, Call as Besef'
HEKEN-EM-BESEF, NIS-EM-BESEF

hTty hTty
HETJETY- HETJETY

ibwi hnw
IBWI HENU

pATT-pATT
PATJETJ-PATJETJ

bsy-bsy
BESY-BESY

Study 2.3

Canopic Jar Formula

Canopic jars were placed in the tomb and contained the internal mummified organs (viscera) of the deceased.

Each one carried a formula for the protection of the viscera which invoked the protection of a goddess for the protection of the jar's contents by one of the four sons of Horus:

Each of the canopic jar spells above starts with the phrase:

Dd mdw in Awsir

'Spoke words by Osiris - name'

Goddess	Son of Horus	Jar Head	Organ
ist 'Isis'	**imsti** 'Imsety'	human	liver
nbt-hwt 'Nephthys'	**Hpy** 'Hapy'	baboon	lungs
nt 'Neith'	**dwA-mwt-f** adore-mother-his 'Duamutef'	jackal	stomach
srqt 'Selkis'	**qbH-snw-f** libation-offerings-his 'Qebhsenuef'	hawk	intestines

Example of a Protection Formula:

Dd mdw, in Ast, Hap awy, Hr nty, im.i, stp-sA, Hr imsti, nty im.i, imsty wsr
speak words, by Isis, secret two-arms, upon that-which, in.me, protection, upon Imseti, who within.me, Imsety Osiris

nsw (ra-xpr-nb) mAa xrw nTr nfr
king (Neb-kheper-u-Ra) true voice god good

'Words spoken by Isis: I place my secret two arms upon that which is within me, protection upon Imsety, who is within me, Imsety (of the) Osiris King, Neb-kheperu-ra, the True of Voice (Justified) good god'

Study 2.4

Funerary Shabty Figures

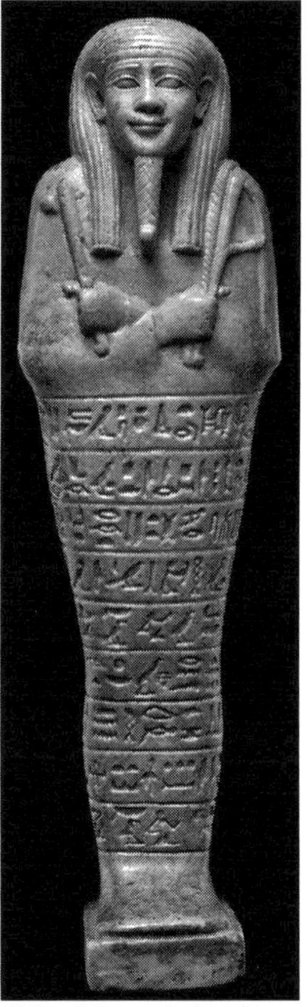

Blue faience shabty figure

Shabty figurines were small statues placed in the tomb to act on behalf of the deceased should they be called upon in the afterlife to do work.

Ushabty in Egyptian means 'answerer' and the Shabty when called would reply 'I am here and will come wherever you bid me.'

Usually inscribed up the shabty figure was a version of Chapter 6 of the Book of the Dead:

Chapter 6 of the Book of the Dead

O shabti figure(s)
If (Name) is called up to do any work that is done there in the underworld
Then the checkmarks (on the work list) are struck for him there
As for a man for his (work service) duty
Be counted yourself at any time that might be done
To cultivate the marsh, to irrigate the riverbank fields
To ferry sand to west or east
'I am doing it – see, I am here', you are to say

The following is an example inscription:

SAbty pn, iry Hsb tw, iry aS tw, ipt m Xrt-nTr

Shabty this, if adjudged one, if call one, decreed in necropolis

r ssrd sxwt, r smHy wDbw, r Xnt Saw, n iAbt, r imntt,

to plant fields, to flood river-banks, to transport sand, from east, to west,

irt.i, mk wi, kA im

do.I, behold I, call therein

'This Shaby, if I be adjudged, if I be called, it is be decreed in the necropolis to plant fields and irrigate river banks or to transport sand from the east to the west, I will do it, I am here to do when you call.'

Study 2.5

The Tomb of Nefertari

Nefertari seated before and playing the game of senet

Awsr nsw, Hmt wrt, nb-tAwy (nfr-itry, mrt-n-mwt)

Osiris king, wife great, lady two-lands (Beautiful-lady, Beloved-of-Mut)

mAa xrw, Awsr nTr aA
true voice, Osiris god great

'Osiris King's Great Wife, Lady of the Two-Lands, Neferitry, beloved of the (mother) goddess Mut, True of Voice (Justified), (judged by) Osiris the Great god.'

The goddess Maat on the lintel of the door to the burial chamber, her wings are outstretched in an act of protection.

Dd mdw, in mAat, sAt ra, xwi sA(t) nsw Hmt wrt (mwt, nfr-itry, n mrt) mAa xrw

speak words, by Maat, daughter of Ra, protector daughter, king wife great
(Neferitry, beloved of Mut) True of Voice

'Words spoken by the goddess Maat, daughter of Ra, daughter protector (of) the King's Great Wife (Neferitry, beloved of Mut) True of Voice.'

Nefertari before the god Thoth

Nefertari comes before the patron god of scribes, Thoth, to receive the scribes palette and pot in order to read and write in the afterlife.

The scribe's palette can be seen placed inside a **wsx** pot, sat on the pot is the **Hqt** sign, the frog goddess Heket. The frog was the symbol of life and fertility and since after the inundation millions of them came to life carries the concept of 'many.'

To the upper right of Nefertari's head is her cartouche and titles: 'King's great wife, Lady of the Two-Lands, Neferitry- Beloved of the goddess Mut, under the great god. To the right over Thoth's head is the following:

Dd mdw, di.n, n xa ra, Dd mdw, di.n, n Ist, imy Dsr

spoken words, given.of, for glorious-appearance Ra, spoken words, given.of,
for Isis, who-is-in land sacred

'Words to be spoken, given to the glorious appearance of Ra,
words to be spoken, given to Isis who is in the Sacred Land'

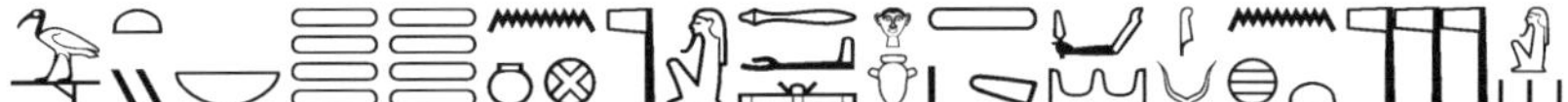

Dwty, nb xmnw, nTr aA, Hr-ib tA-Dsr, Sw-wp, n xt nTrw

Djhwty, lord (of) Hermopolis (Eight-Town), god great, upon-heart (within), land-sacred, truth-judge, of things/affairs gods

'Djhwty, Lord of Hermopolis (Eight Town) of the great god, who is in the midst of the sacred land, judge of truth of the affairs of the gods'

The rest of the text is from Chapter 94 of the Book of the Dead and is entitled: 'The chapter of praying for an ink jar and palette.'

r(A) n dbH, pA wsx, gsty, ma DHwty, m Xrt-nTr

spell for request, the pot, palette from Djhwty in Necropolis

'Utterance for requesting the pot and palette from Djhwty (Thoth) in the Necropolis'

in Awsir nsw Hmt wrt, nbt tAwy (nfr-itry, mrt-n-mwt) mAa-xrw

by Osiris king wife great, lady two-lands (Nefer-itry, beloved of Mut) true-voice

'by the Osiris King's Great Wife, Nerferitry, beloved of Mut, True of Voice'

i wr mAA it iry mDAt n DHwty

hail great-one, see father, keeper papyrus-book of Djhwty

'Hail Great One who sees his father, keeper of the book of Djhwty'

mk wi, ii.kwi, Ax.k, bA.kwi, sxm m nxt.k

behold I, come.I, power-of-god.your, soul.I, mighty with strength.your

'Behold I come with the power of your god, my soul mighty with your strength'

apr.kwi m sSw, DHwty ? ir.i

equipped.i, with writings, Djhwty... [damaged text follows, but reads:]

'and equipped with the writings of Thoth...'

'...bring me the messenger of Akeru (the lion headed earth god) who is with Seth. Bring me the bowl, bring me the palette from that of Thoth, their secrets with them. Gods behold I am a scribe. Bring me the excrement of Osiris, my writings that I may perform the instructions of Osiris, the Great God, perfectly every-day, consisting of the good which you have decreed me. Oh Ra Horakhety, I shall act the truth and shall attain the truth.'

Appendix

Answers to Exercises

1.b

ANSWERS TO EXERCISE 1.b

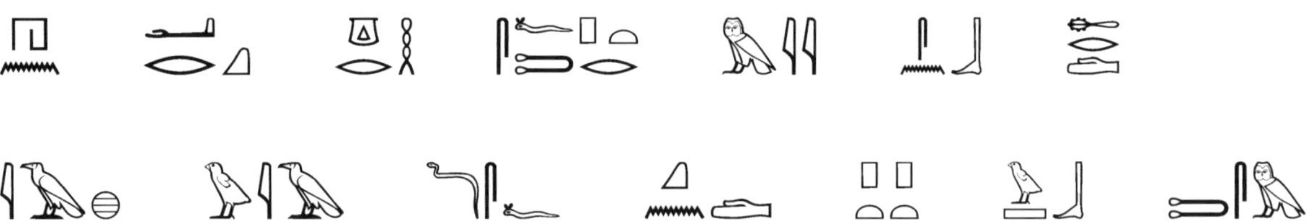

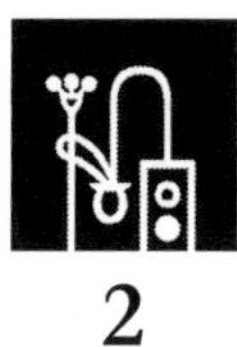

2

ANSWERS TO EXERCISE 2

Transliterate and translate:

1. **wbn ra, m axt** rises Ra, in horizon 'Ra rises in the horizon'

2. **Dd s, gr st** speaks man, silent woman '(when) a man speaks, the woman is silent'

3. **xd sS, m dpt, r niwt tn** fare-downstream scribe, in boat, to town this 'the scribe fares downstream in a boat to this town'

4. **sDm sS pn, n ptH** hear scribe this, to Ptah 'this scribe listens to Ptah'

5. **iw ra, m pt, Hna iaH** behold/is sun, in sky, together with moon 'the sun is in the sky together with the moon'

6. **xm sS, ky sxr** know-not scribe, another plan 'the scribe does not know another plan'

7. **hA dpt tn, r S, iw niwt, m rSwt** go-down boat this, to lake, behold/is town, in joy ‘(When) this boat goes down to the lake, the town is in joy’

8. **sDm nDs pn, rn** hear poor-man this, name ‘this poor man hears the name’

9. **iw ky s, m pr pn** is another man, in house this ‘another man is in this house’

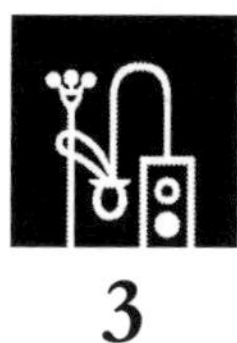

3

ANSWERS TO EXERCISE 3

Transliterate and translate:

1. **Dd.Tn, rn.Tn, n sS pn** say.you, name.yours, to scribe this 'you say your name to this scribe'

2. **mAA s, sAt.f, m pr.f, iw.f, m rSwt** see man, daughter.his, in house.his, is.he, in joy '(when) the man sees his daughter in his house, he is in joy'

3. **DA ra pt, m wiA.f** ferry-across ra heaven, in sacred-bark.his 'the sun god Ra ferries across the heavens in his sacred boat'

4. **hAb it, sA.f, r niwt, Dd.f, sxr n sS** send father, son.his, to town, say.he, plan to scribe 'the father sends his son to the city, that he may say the plan to the scribe'

5. **ix sDm.k, sHtA pn** then hear.you, secret this 'then you will hear this secret'

6. **rS TAty, mAA.f, Hr.s** rejoice vizier, sees.he, face.hers 'the vizier rejoices, when he sees her face'

7. **Dd ptH, m r(A).f, Ds.f** says Ptah, with mouth.his, himself 'Ptah speaks with his own mouth'

8. **iw.T, m bAkt.i** is/are.you, as maid-servant.my 'you are my maid-servant'

9. **hAb.tw, bAk, r niwt, Hr kAt tn** send.one, man-servant, to city, concerning work this 'the man-servant is sent to the city, concerning this work'

4

ANSWERS TO EXERCISE 4

Transliterate and translate:

1. 

nfr sA, sDm.f, n it.f, iw.f, m Xrd, di.f, sxr pn, m ib.f, sxA.f sw, hrw nb, mk.tw, Dd.tw r.f, Sw sw, m Dw nbt

good son, hears.he, to father.his, is/are he, as child, places.he, counsel this, in heart.his, remembers.he it, day every, behold.one, says.one, concerning.him, free he, from evil all

'The good son he listens to his father,(when) he is a child, he places this counsel in his heart, he remembers it every day, behold, one says about him, he is free from all evil'

2.

xa ra, m Axt, wbn.f, m pt, nfr ib nb, mAA.sn, sw

appear sun, in horizon, shine.it, in sky, happy heart all, see they, it

'the sun appears in the horizon and it shines in the sky, happy in heart are all when they see it'

3.  **bin.wy, itrw, Sw m mw**

evil.double, river, empty from water 'very evil is a river, when empty of water'

4. **Dd.k, st, n ity, ix Dd.f, n bAk.f, m-mitt** say.you, it, to sovereign, then says.he, to servant.your, likewise 'you speak it to the sovereign, then he will likewise speak to the servant'

5. **aA.wy, pr.k, aSA sw, m xt nbt, nfrt** great.dual, house.your, abundant it, with things all, beautiful 'how great is your house, it is rich in every beautiful thing'

6. **xm.f, sxr pn, iqr** know-not.him, plan this, excellent 'he does not know this excellent plan'

7. **hAb.sn, dpt r niwt, dA.f, Tw im.s** send.they, boat to city, ferry-across.it, you in.it 'they send a boat to the city, it ferries you across in it.'

5

ANSWERS TO EXERCISE 5

1.

iw grt, rdi.n.i, t, n Hqr, Hnqt n ib, Hbs n Hay

behold now, give.of.i, bread to hungry, beer to thirsty, clothes to naked

'Behold now, I gave bread to the hungry, beer to the thirsty and clothes to the naked.'

2. 

hAb.n, wi, nb.i, r kmt, in.n.i, n.f, xt nbt nfrt, im

send.of, me, lord.my, to Egypt, bring.of.i, to him, things all beautiful, therefrom

'My lord sent me to Egypt, I brought to him every good thing therefrom'

3.

iw nsw, m pr.f, mi ra, m pt

behold/is king, in house.his, like Ra, in sky

'The king is in his house like Ra in the sky'

4. 

ix, di.T, DA.n(w), Tn r Xnw

then, make.you, ferry-across.we, you to residence
'Then you cause us to ferry you across to the residence' ie 'you made us ferry you across to the residence'

5. 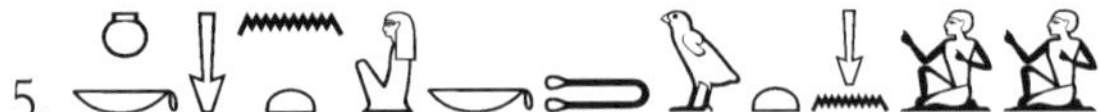

ink, snt.k, Tw sn.i

I-am, sister.your, you brother.my

'I am you sister, you are my brother'

6.

gm.n, sw, Hmt tn, Hr wAt, di.n.s, n.f, t Hnqt

found.of him, woman this, upon road, give.of.her, to.him, bread beer

'This woman found him upon the road, she gave to him bread and beer'

7. 

Dd n.n, wAb ib.f say to.us, priest heart.his 'The priest tells us his heart (wish)'

8.

iw, in.Hm, aA, di.n.f, sw, Hr sA.f

bring.of.slave, donkey, place.of.him, he, upon back.its

'The slave brought the donkey, he placed him-(self) upon its back'

9. 

di.n.sn, hA bAkt, r itrw

make.they, go-down maid-servant, to river

'They made the maid-servant go down to the river'

6

ANSWERS TO EXERCISE 6

1. 

iw, dbH.n.f, n.f mu, iw, rdi.n.sn, n.f irtt

behold, ask.of.him, for.him water, behold, give.of.them, to.him milk

Behold, he asked for him(self) water, behold, they gave to him milk

'He begged water for himself and they gave him milk'

2. 

iw, xAswt nbt, Xr rdwy.f

behold/is/are, foreign-countries all, under (two)feet.his

'All foreign countries are under his feet'

3. 

di.tw, n.f, a, Hr wAwt, imntwt give.one, of.he, hand, upon ways, western 'He is given a hand upon the western ways

4. 

mH aAw.f, r.sn, m it

fill.of donkeys.his, mouth.their, m barley

'His donkeys filled their mouths with barley'

5. 

nt.Tn(w), Xrdw.i

of/belonging-to.you, children.my

'You are my children'

6. 

ix, di nTr.i, niwty, Sm rdwy.i

then, give-cause god.my, local-god, go-depart two-feet.my

'Then, my local god will cause my feet to walk'

7. 

iw, rmT(t) nbt, Xr rSwt, mAA.sn(w), mr pn, aA

is/are, men all, under joy, see.they, pyramid this great

'All men are in joy when they see this great pyramid'

8. 

di.n, TAty, Dd.s, imt ib.s, nbt cause/made.of vizier say.she, being-in heart.hers, all

'The vizier made her say all that was in her heart'

9.

iw, tAS.f, iAbty r itrw, imnty.f, r niwt tn

is, boundary.his, eastern to river, western.his, to town this

'His eastern boundary is at the river, his western is at this town'

10. 

iw nHH, m Hr.f, mi hrw

is eternity, in sight.his, like day

'Eternity is in his sight is like a day'

7

ANSWERS TO EXERCISE 7

b) Transliterate and translate:

1. 

ix, di.Tn(w), rn.i, m r, n Hmw.Tn(w)

then, place.you, name.my, in mouth, of slaves.your

'Then you place my name in the mouth of your slaves,'

sxAw.i, xr msw, nw msw.Tn(w)

memory.my, with children, of children.your

'my memory with the children of your children'

2. 

iw, st.n.i, mw, n it.i, mwt.i, m niwt.sn(w), nt nHH

behold, pour.of.i, water, for father.my, mother.my, in town.their, of eternity

'Behold, I poured water for my father (and) my mother in their town of eternity.'

3.

i, nTrw im(y)w dwAt, ink, mAa-xrw, Sw m isft

O, gods who-are-in underworld, I-am, true-voice, free from wrongdoing

'O, gods who are in the underworld, I am True of Voice and free from wrongdoing'

4. 

iw, Hswt.k, m nsw-pr

is/are, praises.your, in king-house

'Your praises are in the palace'

5. 

di.n Ra, nxt kmt, r tAw nb(w)

given.of Ra, victory Egypt, over lands all

'Ra gave Egypt victory over all lands'

6. 

pri.n, nsw sA pn, m sbA, n pr.f go-out.of, king son this, from door house.his

'The king's son went out of the door of his house'

7.

mk.n(w), m bAkwt, nt mwt.k

behold.we, in-theposition-of maid-servants, of mother.your

'Behold we are maid servants of your mother'

8. 

ir.n.f, wi, m TAty, m niwt.f, rsy

made.of.he, I as vizeier, in town.his, southern

'He made me vizier in his southern town'

8

ANSWERS TO EXERCISE 8

Transliterate and translate:

1. 

n, nDnD.i, Hna Dw, qd

not, converse.I, together-with evil, character-one

'I did not converse together with one of evil character'

2. 

mH.n, Hmw.f, Snwt, m it aSA, nn Dr

fill.of, slaves.his, granary, with corn many, not end

'his slaves filled the granary with plenty of corn, without end'

3. 

iw, rdi.n wi, Hm n nsw-bit (ra-s-Htp-ib) m HAty-a, n niwt.i

behold, gave.to me, majesty of King-Upper-Lower-Egypt (Ra-S-hetep-ib) in-the-position-of ruler, of town.my

'Behold, the Majesty of the King of Upper and Lower Egypt, S-hetep-ib-ra gave me the position, ruler of my town'

4. 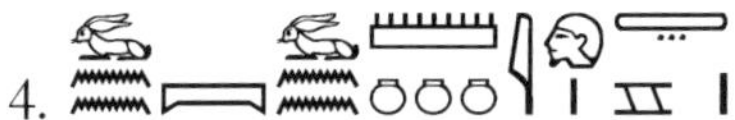

wnn pt, wnn mnw.i, tp ta

exist heaven, exist monument.my, upon land
'as long as heaven shall exist, my monument shall exist upon the earth'

5. 

n sp, irt mitt, in bityw, Dr rk nTr

not happen, do like, by kings-Lower-Egypt, since time god

'never has the like been done by the kings of Lower Egypt, since the time of the god'

6. 

nn mhy.i, Hr sxr nb, n nb.i

not careless.I, concerning plan any, of lord.my

'I shall not be careless concerning any plan of my lord'

7. 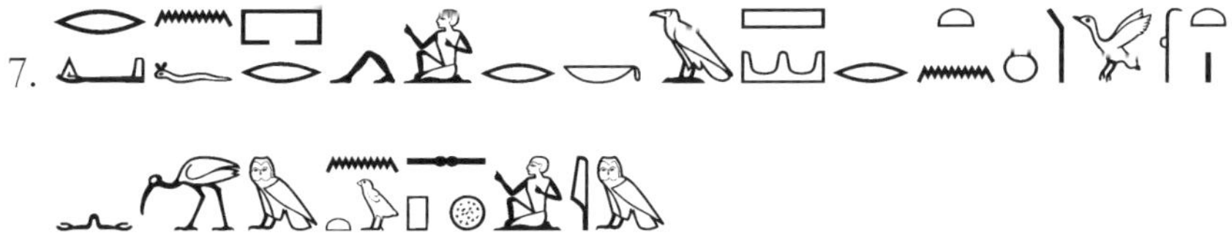

rdi.n.f, pr.i, r kAS, r tnw rnpt, n, gm.n.tw, sp.i, im

cause.of.he, go-up.I, to Cush, for every year, not, find.of.one, fault.my, therein

'he made me to go up to Kush every year and no fault of mine was found there'

8.

iw, in.n, nTr-Hm pn, sS, m iqr bit, nn wn, mitw.f, m tA pn, r Dr.f

behold, bring.of, god-slave this, scribe, as excellent qualities, not exist, equal.his, in land this, to end.its

'this priest brought the scribe, who was excellent of qualities, there was not his equal in this entire land'

9.

rid.n.sn(w), n.s nhy, n t Hnkt

give.of.them, of her little, of bread beer

'they gave to her a little of bread and beer'

9

ANSWERS TO EXERCISE 9

b) Transliterate and translate:

1. 

ntf HqA, Dt nb, nHH of-he (belonging to him), ruler everlasting, lord eternity

'He is the ruler of the everlasting and lord of eternity'

2. 

Dd.Tn(w), n.i, rn n, nTr pf aA, imy pr pn

say.you, to.me, name of, god that great, who-is-in house this
'You say to me the name of that great god who is in this house'

3. 

iw, nn n aAw, n imy-r, pr wr

behold, these of donkeys, of overseer house great
'These donkeys belong to the great overseer of the house'

4. 

iw, di.n.f, Dd st HAty-a, n sAt, nt TAty

behold, made.of.he, say it mayor, to daughter, of vizier
'He made the mayor to say it to the daughter of the vizier'

5. **nn, n.k, mw** not, to.you, water 'You have no water'

6.

Sm.n, nAy.s, n bAkw, wa nb, r st iry

go.of, her, of servants, one any, to place thereof

'Her servants went, each one to the assigned (thereof) place'

7. 

ntf, tAw nb, n.f, imy pt

belongs-to-him, lands all, to.him, therein heaven

'To him belong all the lands, to him belongs the heavens'

8.

iw, in.n, nA n wrw, nw XAswt, Xrdw.sn(w), Hna.sn(w)

behold, bring.of, these of great-ones, of foreign-lands, children.their, together-with.them

'Behold, the great ones of foreign lands brought their children with them'

9. 

ntk, nxt a, n aHa-n, ky, m-hAw.k

you, strong arm, not stand-up, another, in-neighbourhood-of.you

'You are mighty of arm no other can stand up against you'

10

ANSWERS TO EXERCISE 10

Transliterate and translate:

1.

iw, Sms.n.i, Hm.f, Hr rdwy.i, ti sw, Hr xAst tn

behold, follow.of.i, majesty.his, upon feet.my, now/when he, upon foreign-country this

'I followed His Majesty upon my feet, when he was in (upon) this foreign country'

2. 

sb.k nHH, m nDm-ib, m Hswt, nTr imy.k, wnn HAty.k, nn bT.f, tw

pass.you eternity, in happiness, in praises, god who-is-in.you, exist heart.you, together-with.you, not forsake.you, one/it

'You shall pass eternity in happiness, and in praises of the god who is in you, your heart shall be with you, it will not forsake you'

3. 

mk, niwt tn, m Hb, iw.k, m nb.s

behold, town this, in festival, is/are.you, as lord.its

'Behold this town is in festival, now that you are its lord'

4. 

nn iw, n nTr, r.i

not wrong/crime, to god, concerning.i

'There is no crime to the god in respect of me'

5. 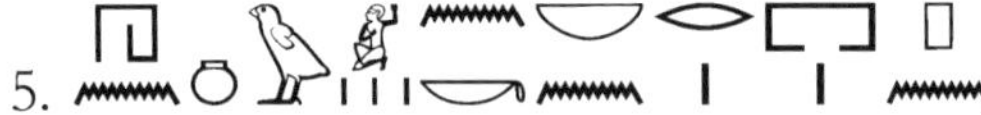

hnw n.k, nb n r-pr, pn

praises to.you, lord of temple.this

'Praises are to you, lord of this temple'

6. 

iw, Apd aA, Hr xt pn, qA

is bird great, upon tree this, high

'A great bird is upon this high tree'

7. 

iw, km.n.i, hrw aSa, isT wi, m wab, imy Abd.f

behold, complete.of.i, days many, lo I, as priest, who-is-in month.his

'I completed many days while I was the priest who is in his month'

8. 

mk, sy Hna.k

behold, she together-with.you

'Behold, she is with you'

9. 

HA.n.i, nhy n t

would-that/wish.of.i, little of bread

'Wish I had a little bread'

10. 

wnn Xrdw.Tn(w), Hr nswt.Tn(w)

exist/be children.your, upon seats.your

'Your children shall be upon your seats'

ARK PUBLISHING

Ameni-amenna

Made in United States
Orlando, FL
28 August 2023